17 Felony Charges:
NOT GUILTY

Priscilla E. Oates
(Former Mayor, Town of Princeville NC)
Terms:
2002-2005
2010-2013

Elite
PUBLICATIONS

An Elite Publications Book
2120 E Firetower Rd. # 107-58
Greenville, NC 27858
Tel: 919-618-8075
info@elitepublications.org
www.elitepublications.org

17 Felony Charges: Not Guilty Second Edition
All Rights Reserved. Published in 2025 by Elite Publications
Copyright © 2025 Priscilla E. Oates
Second Edition Printing: January 2025

PAPERBACK ISBN-13: 979-8-218-58473-3

HARDCOVER ISBN-13: 979-8-218-58474-0

KINDLE & EBOOK ISBN-13: 979-8-218-58475-7

PRINTED IN THE UNITED STATES OF AMERICA

Dedication

*This is dedicated to my loving husband,
Duarthur Oates, Sr., who has supported me
in this journey all the way!*

Acknowledgements

I would like to thank...

My husband, Duarthur Oates Sr, my son, Duarthur Oates, II

To my late mother & father, Maggie Lee Everette & Julius Everette, Sr.

To all my family members who supported and encouraged me.

To my awesome legal Dream Team led by: Attorney Charles Bonner, Attorney Ryan Stump, Attorney Samuel Randall

Attorney Charles Watts, II

Attorney Malvern King

Attorney Joe Hester

Former Mayor Pro-tem Isabelle Purvis-Andrews

Former Interim Manager, Maggie Boyd

Former Town Clerk, Daisy Staton

Congressman G.K. Butterfield (Retired)

Former Mayor William Bell of Durham, NC (Retired)

Reginald Smith

Kim Powell-Baker

17 Felony Charges: NOT GUILTY

Dr. Alma Hobbs, Former Asst. Secretary US Dept of Agriculture

Dr. Jeffrey Harris & Pastor Gwendolyn Harris (Florence, SC)

The late Dr. Frank & Jonell Summerfield (Raleigh, NC)

Pastor Mitchell Summerfield (Raleigh, NC)

Pastor Willie Mae Bryant (Tarboro, NC)

Thema Smith, Xpozure Studio

To every prayer warrior who prayed and interceded on my behalf. I thank you and I love each of you!

To the following pastors: Rev. Roosevelt Higgs, Rev. Thomas Walker, Rev. George Terry, Rev. Richard Joyner & Rev. Jonah Walston – each of these pastors signed a petition and gave it to D.A. Robert Evans to release me. They knew I was innocent. God's abundant blessings to you all!

Community Pastor Leaders

Special thanks to Bishop T.D. Jakes whose sermons and message helped me stay focused on the Word of God and keep my faith strong!

17 Felony Charges: NOT GUILTY

Table of Contents

Introduction: I Found Out What It Was 11

1: History of Princeville, NC 19

2: Princeville Economic Development........................23

3: Attorney Charles Bonner........................67

4: Judge Osmond Smith's Order 79

5: T. Vance Holloman 83

6: Beth Wood 125

7: Barry Long 145

8: SBI/Agent Lolita Chapman 161

9: Attorney Malvern King 179

10: Affidavits & Declarations........................191

11: Tonya Montanye........................227

12: God Gets ALL the Glory! 247

References 252

About the Author 253

17 Felony Charges: NOT GUILTY

Introduction

Power, greed and control can make people do things that are downright unthinkable. It all comes down to this -- They do what they want to do when they're on that level. It takes God to catch them. It was a group of North Carolina (NC) elected, head-of-state officials who led the allegations and indictments against me.

Thinking back on everything that transpired I can only shake my head and thank God for keeping me and giving me the strength to endure. I don't wish this on my worst enemy. Unless you have experienced something like this, I cannot explain what it's like to be blatantly and outright falsely accused and indicted by people who knew from the start that they were setting me up to cover up their crooked schemes.

My heart was so heavy... the many nights I couldn't sleep... the tears that rolled down my cheeks each time I thought about what I was going through. I believe God really let me see what pure evil looks like. These people were purely evil and corrupt. I asked myself many times, "What did I do to deserve this?" I prayed and asked God to show me what was going on.

Walking into the court room, then hearing the judge tell me I had been indicted. My heart felt like it stopped beating and the breath left my lungs. Were those words correct? He just said I was facing 75 years... YEARS... in prison for crimes I absolutely did NOT commit? I believe I know what Jesus felt like on the cross. "Father, forgive them for know not what they are doing." It is a feeling I will never forget and one I cannot describe accurately in words.

I was literally arrested.

I wasn't ready.

Nothing could have prepared me.

Who is Priscilla Everette-Oates?

I was born in Edgecombe County, Princeville, North Carolina. My mother's name was Maggie Lee Everette and my father's name was Julius Everette, Sr. I'm the youngest of 13 children. We were a close-knit family and we lived in a 3-bedroom house... four brothers in one room and my sisters in another room and I always slept with my mom.

I didn't actually sleep by myself until I went to college at NC A&T State University where I majored in Accounting, and I was the first one of all my siblings to graduate from college. Thinking back, there may have been a few times that I had the bed to myself when my brothers and sisters moved out, but other than that, I was used to sharing everything.

Growing up I never saw poverty or was aware of it because my mother always had a garden and she raised pigs and chickens. Even though my mother was on welfare, it never felt like we were poor. Both my parents worked and I learned to work hard and have compassion for others.

I accepted Jesus Christ in my late 20s and that helped me find my passion and purpose which is helping people at risk, on drugs and coming from broken families. Most of all, my passion is leading souls to Jesus Christ. I am the founder of a non-profit organization and owner of behavioral health care organizations focusing on mental health and substance abuse which involves holistic treatments.

Why I ran for mayor...

In 2002, I ran for mayor because God spoke to me in such a way that I knew it was Him. Literally. There was a pressing... an urgency from the Holy Spirit that told me this was something I had to do. Even though I had no interest in politics and I wasn't even thinking about doing something like this, I felt very strong that someone needed to be the voice for Princeville.

I was appointed as a Commissioner in 2000 and when the position for mayor came up in 2002, I ran and I won. Prior to being appointed as Commissioner, I was aware that the financial books had been taken from Princeville in 1997 and everything was in an uproar. I knew someone had to step in and do something to get the city back on track.

17 Felony Charges: NOT GUILTY

What this book is about...

This book is about how the enemy worked through North Carolina (NC) government officials to falsely accuse, indict me, and attempt to send me to prison for over 75 years for crimes I did not commit when I was mayor of the oldest town chartered by Blacks in 1885 -- Princeville, North Carolina. I am going to share the details with you in hopes that you, the reader, are able to see a few things: corruption, conspiracy, concealment and fabrication from the NC LGC (Local Government Commission), SBI (State Bureau of Investigations), and the NC Office State Auditors (OSA).

First, my prayer is that you see the power and goodness of God. When He is on your side, there is no battle you will lose. Second, I want you to see what happens when power is given to certain head officials and it is misused. Greed, control, domination, corruption... those are just a few of the things that I experienced and I will share.

BRIEF NARRATIVE...

Part 1: The Accusation

In 2013, a shadow descended over the historic town of Princeville, North Carolina. A place founded by freed slaves, Princeville was now at the center of a legal storm that would threaten to bury its vibrant legacy under false accusations and political maneuvering. At the heart of it stood Mayor Priscilla Everette-Oates, a woman of deep faith, boundless community service, and unwavering dedication to the town she had been twice elected to serve. The accusations, however, painted a different picture—one of deceit, embezzlement, and betrayal.

It began with a press release from the State of North Carolina, charging Mayor Oates with 17 felony counts of embezzlement of public funds. The staggering accusation claimed that she had misused a mere $5,200 over the course of three years. Each felony carried a sentence of 4 ½ years in state prison, amounting to a potential 75-year sentence. For a woman who had spent her life serving others, it seemed an impossible reality. Yet, the State, along with the Local Government Commission (LGC), OSA (Office of State Auditors), and the State Bureau of Investigation (SBI), insisted on her guilt.

But the truth, as it would slowly come to light, was that these allegations were not merely a misstep—they were a deliberate act of political assassination.

Part 2: The Evidence Buried
As Mayor Oates' legal ordeal began, the LGC and SBI took swift action. The LGC seized documents and receipts from the town of Princeville, records that held the key to her innocence. Charles Bonner, Ryan Stump, and Samuel Randall, her legal Dream Team, quickly realized that this evidence—these very receipts—proved that Mayor Oates had never used public funds for personal gain. She had always acted in the best interest of the town.

Incredibly, despite having evidence of her innocence in their possession, the LGC, OSA (Office of State Auditor) and SBI chose to bury it. They refused repeated legal requests from the defense to release the receipts. Mayor Oates' attorneys sent letter after letter, subpoena after subpoena, demanding the documents.

Even a Freedom of Information Act request was filed, all to no avail. The LGC and SBI were steadfast in their refusal, tightening the noose around an innocent woman.

Months passed. As the threat of a 75-year prison sentence loomed over her head, Mayor Oates watched in disbelief. The system, designed to protect her, seemed bent on destroying her.

Part 3: The Struggle for Justice
Her legal Dream Team would not relent. A breakthrough came when Judge W. Osmond Smith III issued a stern court order. It was a scathing rebuke of the LGC's refusal to comply with legal procedures, demanding that they finally hand over the receipts proving Oates' innocence. Faced with this ultimatum, the LGC begrudgingly submitted the documents they had hidden for so long.

The evidence was undeniable. Mayor Oates had never taken a single cent for herself. Every dollar was used to better the town of Princeville. The dream of her political enemies—to see her silenced and imprisoned—began to unravel.

When District Attorneys Tonya Montanye and Robert Evans saw the evidence, they made a courageous decision. In the face of political pressure and a long-standing narrative of guilt, they dismissed all 17 felony charges. The weight of the accusations that had plagued Oates for years finally lifted.

Part 4: The Aftermath
The ordeal was over, but the damage was done. It was clear to all that the prosecution had not been about justice. As her attorney Charles Bonner declared, it had been a political assassination. Her enemies, those who sought to undermine her efforts for economic

development and growth in Princeville, had orchestrated the entire ordeal. But they had underestimated her resilience.

Mayor Oates emerged from the trial not as a defeated politician, but as a beacon of hope for her community. With her name cleared, she returned to her lifelong work of service. She and her husband, both ordained ministers, continued their work feeding the hungry through their food bank—a project they had maintained for over a decade.

But her vision for Princeville had grown beyond immediate relief. Mayor Oates set her sights on the future. She resumed her plans for economic development, determined to lift Princeville from its past struggles. A key piece of this vision was the creation of a Bioelectricity Generating Plant, a forward-thinking project that would bring in approximately $250,000 of revenue annually to the town. This was more than just an economic boost—it was a symbol of Princeville's resilience and its capacity to thrive despite the challenges of its past.

Part 5: A Legacy of Resilience

The story of Mayor Priscilla Everette-Oates is not just about false accusations or political intrigue. It is a narrative of resilience, faith, and an unwavering commitment to serve. Despite the attempt to destroy her reputation, Oates' spirit remained unbroken. Her love for Princeville and its people, combined with her deep belief in justice, carried her through the darkest moments of her life.

As she stepped back into the public arena, her resolve was stronger than ever. She thanked the loyal supporters who had stood by her throughout the ordeal and made it clear that her mission to uplift Princeville was far from over.

17 Felony Charges: NOT GUILTY

The political enemies who had tried to erase her legacy had failed. Instead, they had only fortified the narrative of a leader who, despite every effort to silence her, would continue to fight for her community, her faith, and her vision for a better future.

Epilogue: The Fight for Truth

The tale of Mayor Oates is more than a singular story. It reflects broader themes—of justice delayed but not denied, of the power of political forces to distort truth, and of the incredible strength it takes to stand firm in the face of overwhelming opposition. It is a disposition that speaks to the heart of public service, reminding us of all that integrity and resilience are the foundations upon which true leadership is built.

Her story serves as a testament to the enduring fight for truth, justice, and the preservation of one's legacy against all odds.

1.

History of Princeville, NC

Princeville, North Carolina is the very first all-Black incorporated town in the United States in February 1885. This historical town is part of Edgecombe County and the NC Metropolitan Statistical Area. It is physically located on the opposite side of the Tar River, which has a history of flooding, and caused the town many problems during heavy rains and storms. The most catastrophic flood was in 1999 when Hurricane Floyd destroyed pretty much the entire town. Repeated requests for more than 100 years have been made to build a levy to help protect the town, but nothing has been done. Finances have been provided to many NC towns, but Princeville was always overlooked. Residents rebuild and do their best to move forward, even though it appears that they are being treated like red-headed stepchildren.

In 1865 when the Union soldiers defeated the South in the Civil War, more than 4 million Black slaves were given their freedom but they needed to establish their own land and find places to live and settle. A group of freed slaves found an area of swamp land along the Tar River near Edgecombe County where Whites didn't want to live but it was close enough to Tarboro that the Blacks could still come and work for them. Since the Whites didn't want it, they offered it to the Blacks and they called it "Freedom Hill," taken from a mound of land that Whites would address the Blacks from.

17 Felony Charges: NOT GUILTY

About 20 years after establishing Freedom Hill and starting their new "free" lives, a group of Blacks went to Congress to ask for a charter for their town. They were able to educate themselves in the laws and present their case. Originally, their request was rejected as Congress wanted the area named after President James Garfield. The group of Blacks did not agree and pushed back. Eventually, they won and in 1885 became incorporated as Princeville. It was named after Turner Prince who was a carpenter from Pitt County that helped build some of the homes in Freedom Hill and Tarboro.

Unfortunately, due to the swamp lands, flooding did not take the residents by surprise, but they had nowhere else to go so they learned to survive as best they could. A major flood hit the town in 1867 shortly after it was incorporated and years after that as well.

In 1965, the State of North Carolina and the Army Corps of Engineers constructed a dike around the town and that stopped the constant flooding. Since then the community has been hit with four major floods the last was Hurricane Floyd in September 1999. Hurricane Floyd dumped heavy rain on the town causing the dike to breach. The city's 2,100 residents, many of them descendants of the original settlers, found their homes submerged under water. They lost virtually everything.

HISTORIC PRINCEVILLE
★ ★ ★
From Slavery to Freedom Hill

During the Civil War, thousands of slaves escaped to U.S. Army lines, and more than thirty African Americans from Edgecombe County enlisted in the 35th, 36th, and 37th U.S. Colored Troops, 14th U.S. Colored Heavy Artillery, and U.S. Navy. After the war, former slaves sought refuge at a U.S. Army camp located here on the plantations of John Lloyd and Lafayette Dancy. The freedmen called their settlement of huts and shanties on the Tar River floodplain Freedom Hill.

Freedman Turner Prince, a carpenter born into slavery in 1843, acquired a lot here in 1873, built a house, and constructed other permanent dwellings for the residents. By 1880, the population was 379; occupation categories included laborer, laundress, washerwoman, carpenter, blacksmith,

Princeville residential area in the same early 20th century. - Courtesy N.C. Office of Archives and History

Princeville grocery store, commercial area, early 20th century. - Courtesy NC Office of Archives and History

grocer, seamstress, and brick mason. In 1885, the North Carolina legislature incorporated the town, which its occupants named Princeville in their carpenter's honor. Princeville was the first all-black town and independently governed African American community incorporated in the United States.

The town struggled to survive during the Jim Crow era, defeating efforts early in the twentieth century to annex it to Tarboro. Princeville's population increased to 636 by 1910, then declined as black Southerners migrated north. The population later rose to 2,100 in the 1990s.

Princeville's location has subjected it to frequent flooding. A levee completed in 1965 protected the town until 1999, when Hurricanes Dennis and Floyd overtopped it in the worst flood on record here. Princeville's residents soon began rebuilding their historic community, repairing houses and constructing new homes, a town hall, a park, and an African American history museum.

"Coming into the Lines," by combat artist Edwin Forbes, shows escaped slaves passing two Union soldiers. Courtesy Library of Congress

Brothers in Arms. Courtesy Library of Congress

By the 1900s Princeville was a thriving community with stores and businesses which allowed them to be self-sufficient. Residents didn't have to cross the bridge into Tarboro unless they were working. There have been issues with White supremacy that threatened the dissolution of the town, but the residents resisted and stood strong to fight against it.

Hurricane Floyd devastated the town in September 1999 when it hit as a category 3 hurricane. Approximately 20 feet of floodwater covered the town and damaged more than 8,000 homes and also uprooted more than 100 coffins from cemeteries. Hurricane Dennis had also hit NC about a week before Floyd which caused the levee to break. The Tar River swelled to over 40 feet above its normal levels, so the water had nowhere to go but into Princeville. Federal financial assistance was granted to help the residents rebuild; however, the majority of the funds were never received by the town.

2.

Princeville Economic Development

During my administration, one of my primary goals was to rebuild Princeville. I created an Economic Development Committee to help me carry out the ideas and things I wanted to do for the town. We had a vision; we had concrete plans to make Princeville sustainable and desirable for not just living but for doing business to bring in revenue.

The LGC continued saying this Economic Development Committee did not exist. The below documents show our vision statement and some of the projects that were completed along with ideas for the future. They are all taken directly from the Princeville Comprehensive Economic Development Plan.

VISION:

The town of Princeville Strategic Plan offers a unique opportunity to foster economic opportunity as well as to increase the quality of life in the Town of Princeville, North Carolina.

The residents of Princeville, North Carolina clearly face a broad range of pressing problems — problems that challenge the basic structure of our social and physical environment. While there have been task forces established to study the impact of a substantially reduced tax base, and proposals and counter proposals aimed at the ultimate solution, it is abundantly clear that no easy solution exists.

A serious unabated program of minority economic enfranchisement in the Town of Princeville is worthwhile in its own right as a cure to decades of imbalance in the distribution of federal, state, and local financial resources targeted to benefit the unemployed, the underemployed, and low-income group members. If properly perceived and financially supported, an economic development program with a focus on minorities could play a crucial role in providing leverage in the resolve of economic development programs in the Town of Princeville.

The perennial complaint among minority community based organization and their leadership within the Town of Princeville is their perception that invariably many economic development agencies join with society in condemning the dependency of the economic underclass, while offering no viable alternatives to the dependency. Many of the economic development professional functionaries representing these agencies continually advocate maturity, self-determination, and competence by minority groups and businesses, and, at the same time subject their feeble requests and identification of their real needs to exhaustive scrutiny.

While we assure that minority organizations and businesses with the Town of Princeville should truly represent middle America standards of initiative and responsibility, the system knowingly or unknowingly restricts access to the facilities (banks and other lending institutions) and financial resources likely to foster those virtues beneficial to the group. A number of studies have been conducted that document the deleterious effect of rigid and unrealistic requirements placed on minority community based organizations and businesses with the Town of Princeville. Certainly chronic dependence, apathy, and a primitive unfocused rage are inevitable by-products of a system that fails to recognize that minority organizations and businesses have a right to participate on an "equal basis" in economic development planning and implementation.

PROJECTS ACCOMPLISHED:

May 2010: The very first retail store (Dollar General) opened its doors in Princeville

November 2010: Princeville-Tarboro Bridge over the Tar River

17 Felony Charges: NOT GUILTY

2007: Freedom Hill Clinic – the very first clinic serving Edgecombe & surrounding areas

Photo: courtesy www.cfhcnc.org

Under my administration, the town of Princeville voted to have the FIRST medical clinic brought to the town and the Board voted and named it in 2005. When it officially opened it was a 10,000 square foot healthcare facility built within Princeville jurisdiction zone.

NEW CLINIC

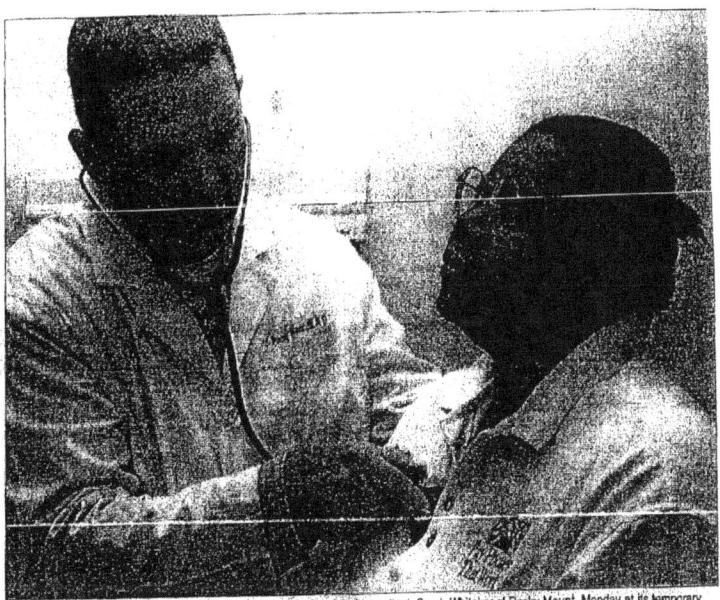

Dr. Bracey Robertson treats Freedom Hill Community Health Center's first patient, Sarah Whitaker of Rocky Mount, Monday at its temporary location in the Tarboro Women's Center building on North Main Street. Photos/Calvin Adkins

The Daily Southerner March 29, 2005

Princeville clinic opens in Tarboro

By CALVIN ADKINS
STAFF WRITER

After nearly two years of planning, the Freedom Hill Community Health Center on Monday saw its first patients at its temporary location in the Tarboro Women's Center building on North Main Street.

Operated by the Carolina Family Health Centers Inc. of Wilson, the health center will offer preventive and primary health care for Edgecombe County residents.

A second temporary facility opened last week in Princeville next to the town hall. The Princeville clinic

Tara Lloyd, eligibility specialist, and Yesenia Cisneros, patient service representative, have been busy making referrals in the Princeville office. 773

including health education, substance abuse and mental health, pharmacy assistance

of opening the center under one roof but adequate space for the operation was not

Princeville and rented space in Tarboro has the operation up and running.

A proposal by Carolina Family Health has been made to build a 4,300 square feet building on 12 acres on North Ridgewood Road in Princeville. Carolina Family Health Executive Director Dee Johnson said engineers are examining the undeveloped property to see if it is durable for the needed infrastructure. If it meets the requirements, construction on the project could be completed within a year, Johnson said.

"We're really excited about the property," she said. "It is very large. We will be able to do lots of things."

The health center is geared towards affordable healthcare for the under-insured, uninsured and low-income residents. However, the center will treat patients regardless

The Daily Southerner
March 29, 2005

Clinic

Continued from front page

billed according to patients' income.

The centers will deliver medical and dental services, provided by a family practice physician, physician assistant/family nurse practitioner, dentist, dental hygienist and nursing and dental assisting staff. Limited mental health and substance abuse services also will be available. Qualifying patients could receive assistance in obtaining affordable prescription medications, also.

"I'm very excited about the opening of the health center," said Mayor Priscilla Everrette-Oates. "This is the first project that I'm aware of that will create 15 permanent jobs in Princeville. It is also the first medical facility to operate in town. History has been made."

Carolina Family Health received a $775,000 federal grant as part of President Bush's 2002 initiative that will add 1,200 new and expanded health centers sites and increase the number of people served annually from about 10 million to 16 million by 2006. Carolina Family Health operates similar health centers in Wilson and Elm City.

The Princeville center will hire 15 employees, at least seven have already been hired.

On Monday the staff at the Tarboro location had a full patient load on its first day

while the Princeville staff has been busy with referrals throughout the week.

"The need was great for a service like this in this area," said Faith Littlejohn, director of operations. "People always look for quality and affordable healthcare, and that is what we offer."

Princeville resident Maxine Lyons was turned away but made an appointment for her grandson for a later date.

"This is good for

Princeville," Lyons said. "We know have a health center that we can call our own."

In an apparent move to make residents feel ownership, Carolina Family Health Board of Directors chose the name Freedom Hill Community Health Center. Freedom Hill was the name given to the town when it was found in 1865. It was incorporated in 1885 and then named Princeville in honor its namesake, Turner

Prince. More than 2,000 people are residents of the town today.

Almost 40 percent of the patients treated at health centers have no insurance coverage and others have inadequate coverage, according to the U.S. Health and Human Services.

Office hours for both locations are 8 a.m. to 5 p.m. Monday - Friday. The telephone number for the Princeville location is 641-1039 and for the Tarboro, 641-0514.

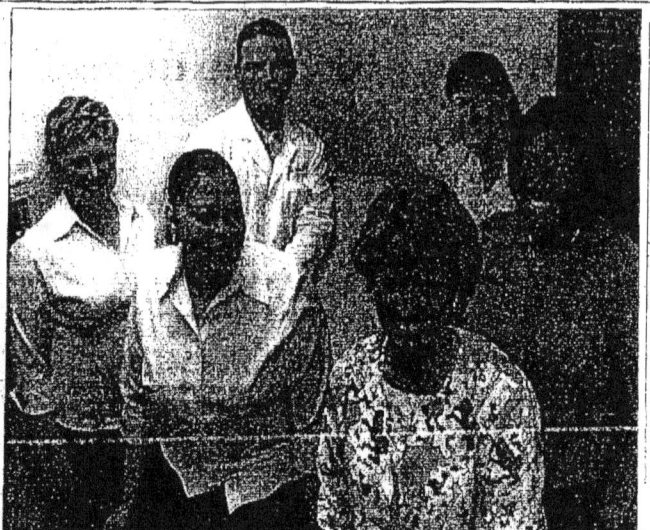

Employees of the Freedom Hill Community Health Center in Princeville are; from left, Ruth Carlon, physician assistant; Faith Littlejohn, director of operations; Dr. Bracey Robertson, physician; Gloria Warwick, nurse; and Tammy Whitehead and Nitkita Dickens, receptionists. Photo/Calvin Adkins

*The Rocky Mount Telegram
Monday, April 4, 2005*

New Princeville health center sees first patients

By JOE MILLER
Staff Writer

TARBORO – Princeville's newest health center is up and running in two different locations.

The Freedom Hill Community Health Center is temporarily operating in the Tarboro Women's Center building next to Heritage Hospital and next to the Princeville Town Hall. The Tarboro site opened March 28 for primary care. The Princeville site opened March 21 for ancillary services, including medication management, substance abuse counseling and health education.

Doctors at the Tarboro site estimated Friday they've seen about 20 patients.

"It's exceeded expectations for the first week," said Paula McMillian, chief financial officer for Carolina Family Health Centers Inc., which operates the center. "We're very pleased with the amount of calls that we got."

Latoya Coward of Conetoe stopped by Friday for a physical and said she likes the Freedom Hill center.

"They're nice (and) fast,"

See CENTER, 2A

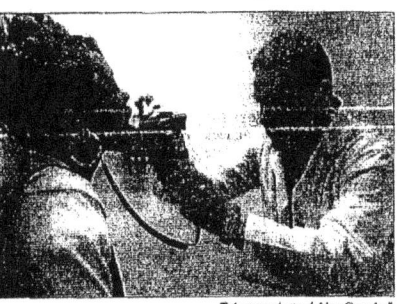

Telegram photo / Alan Campbell

Dr. Bracey Robertson examines Latoya Coward's throat Friday at the Freedom Hill Community Health Center's temporary location at the Tarboro Women's Center.

CENTER

From Page 1A

said Coward, 24.

Money for the new facility came from a $775,000 grant issued by the U.S. Department of Health and Human Services in December. Center officials said they opened both temporary facilities because as a condition of the grant, they couldn't wait to delay the openings.

"They basically gave us four months to open up, and we just were not able to find a site in the Tarboro and Princeville area that was big enough to house both," McMillian said.

A permanent location is planned in Princeville on a 12-acre site off of North Ridgewood Road. McMillian said they have an option to buy the property, but wouldn't say how much they are spending.

"So far, it's looking really good in terms of being a suitable site for our permanent location," she said.

McMillian said she hopes to open the permanent center by May 2006. The facility will house medical and dental facilities, officials said. It will accept all insurance plans, and people without insurance will be placed on a sliding fee scale.

In a previous interview, Princeville Mayor Priscilla Everette-Oates expressed delight over Princeville having its own health center.

"We know that this will provide economic growth, and also, it will increase job opportunity within the town and Edgecombe County," she said.

The Tarboro site is open 8 a.m. to 5 p.m. weekdays except for 9:30 a.m. to 6:30 p.m. on Thursdays. The Princeville site is open 8 a.m. to 5 p.m. weekdays.

17 Felony Charges: NOT GUILTY

PROJECTS PLANNED:

- ➢ Princeville Water Plant – help to solve the town's water issues
- ➢ Wastewater Treatment Center
- ➢ Town-wide Water & Drainage Systems
- ➢ Princeville Post Office
- ➢ Princeville Gymnasium
- ➢ Fast food restaurants
- ➢ Princeville Convention Center (to also include hotel & Cultural Arts Center)
- ➢ Princeville Rehabilitation Center
- ➢ Princeville Financial Institution
- ➢ Princeville Tourism (to also include museum & welcome center)
- ➢ Riverside Heritage Park – which would be the first park for Historic Princeville, NC

We successfully moved forward with the Princeville African American Museum and Heritage Park projects in 2004. See the article below for the groundbreaking ceremony. This was such a wonderful project that came to pass during my administration!

AFRICAN-AMERICAN MUSEUM

ceville Mayor Priscilla Everette-Oates speaks to the dignitaries and guests Tuesday during a groundbreaking ceremony for the Princeville African-American Museum and the Heritage Park Community Center at the site of the old Princeville Town Hall.

Princeville moves foward with projects

By DOROTHY Y. LEWIS
Staff Writer

PRINCEVILLE – Edgecombe County, state and local officials gathered Tuesday for the Heritage Park and Princeville African-American Museum groundbreaking ceremonies.

Heritage Park will be the first recreational community center in the history of the town, said Sam Knight, Princeville town manager.

Knight said the community center will be about 4,500-square feet and have rooms for special events. The park area will have a softball field, picnic tables and a play-

> "The museum will have historical information about Princeville, as well as contain black artifacts from across the state."
>
> **SAM KNIGHT**
> Princeville town manager

ground.

Mayor Priscilla Everette-Oates said she was pleased that the town

would have a place where residents could go.

"The children will have somewhere to play," Everette-Oates said. "The town commissioners and I are working together as a team for more great things in 2004."

Lowe's Home Improvement Warehouse contributed $300,000 for the center, which will be on U.S. 258, Knight said.

"We're hoping the center will be built around March," Knight said. "Barnhill Contractors out of Rocky Mount is working on the construction."

See MUSEUM, 3A

MUSEUM

From Page 1A

Knight said the former town hall on Mutual Boulevard will become known as the Princeville African-American Museum.

"The museum will have historical information about Princeville, as well as contain black artifacts from across the state of North Carolina," Knight said.

Knight said the renovation project for the museum will cost about $360,000.

"It's being funded by the N.C. Department of Transportation and the National Trust Fund," Knight said. He said the museum should open in the latter part of 2004.

Knight said N.C. Sen. Clark Jenkins, D-Edgecombe, was instrumental in the town receiving the needed money for the renovation.

Jenkins said during the ceremony that he is willing to work hard for the people of Princeville and Edgecombe County.

Princeville can be a destination for people to visit, said Edgecombe County Manager Lorenzo Carmon.

"People may be want to come to see how the (1999) flood affected the town and will see that something good came out of something bad," Carmon said.

Please see the below Princeville Progress Reports which highlight just a few of the great accomplishments that were done during my Administration, along with some of the community involvement. We were committed to bringing life and revenue back to Princeville!

I came into office in January 2010 and within one year, the books were in the black! You can see this below in the 4th paragraph of the December 2010 Princeville Progress Report. LGC should have never taken the Princeville books!

17 Felony Charges: NOT GUILTY

December 20, 2010	**PRINCEVILLE PROGRESS REPORT**
	TOWN OF PRINCEVILLE – PRINCEVILLE, NC

HAPPY HOLIDAYS 2010!

PRINCEVILLE PROGRESS REPORT

Contact: **252.823.1057 tel**
            252.823.5388 fax
            www.townofprinceville.org

PRINCEVILLE SWEARS IN NEW CHIEF OF POLICE,
CONTINUES TO IMPROVE THE TOWN'S FINANCIAL CONDITION, and
WELCOMES A NEW EDGECOMBE COUNTY SOCIAL SERVICES JOBS PROGRAM

Mayor Priscilla Everette-Oates, Town Commissioners, and Town management continue to work overtime on re-shaping and re-focusing the resources of the Town of Princeville. Mayor Everette-Oates and Team have accomplished this along with many tasks by bringing the town of the "red" into the "black" budget-wise in the first six (6) months of her newly elected term beginning last December 2009.

The Town of Princeville welcomed a new police chief on Monday, December 13, 2010 at the last Town of Commissioners Meeting. Police Chief Joey Petway was sworn in during the monthly meeting. Chief Petway was formerly employed with the Edgecombe County Sheriff's Office. Petway brings 25 years of law enforcement experience to the post including serving as chief of police with the Enfield Police Department, working on the Charleston City Police Department in Charleston, S.C. and the Rocky Mount City Police Department. Chief Petway is a former U.S. Army Reservist and has completed federal law enforcement training and has received letters of commendation from individuals and businesses for his service.

The Princeville Board of Commissioners adopted the 2010-2011 Fiscal Year Budget and Budget Ordinance. The 2010-2011 Fiscal Year budget is set at **$1,575,122** which represents a decrease in spending of **$368,835** from the 2009-2010 Fiscal Year budget. Therefore, from December 2009 until now, spending has been decreased by $368,835 or 23% of last year's operating budget.

In addition, the North Carolina Department of the State Treasurer has also analyzed the audited financial statements for the Town of Princeville for the year that ended June 30, 2010. The analysis noted that the town has made progress in a number of areas. The NC Department of State Treasurer also noted that audited financial statements were submitted on a timely basis for the second consecutive year, the Town's General Fund balance available increased, and the financial position of the Water and Sewer Fund has improved. The Town's governing board of commissioners, staff, and citizens were commended for these improvements. Significant work continues on improving the Town's financial condition and operations. One

PRINCEVILLE PROGRESS REPORT

December 20, 2010

TOWN OF PRINCEVILLE – PRINCEVILLE, NC

important change was the Town's negative 0.61% at June 30, 2009 which has increased to a positive 15.85% at the June 30, 2010. Town leadership continues to work on areas of improvement necessary to move Princeville into a solid position of strength.

The Town of Princeville and the Edgecombe Department of Social Services have teamed up to offer Princeville citizens the opportunity to apply to the Job Booster grant project underway through the Edgecombe Department of Social Services. The program mirrors the existing Work First initiative and your eligibility will be determined by the Edgecombe Department of Social Services. There is a maximum income and the presence of a school age child in the home requirement for eligibility.

How to Apply: Applications are taken during the hours of 7:30 a.m - 5:30 p.m. Monday through Thursday and 7:30 a.m. -5:00 p.m. on Friday for the Tarboro or Rocky Mount Branch offices.

What you will need: Birth Certificates, Social Security Cards, Identification, Previous Months Pay Stubs, Health Insurance Card, Most Recent Bank Statements, Life Insurance Policies, Alien-INS documentation. The names, addresses, date of birth, and social security number of Absent Parent.

HAPPY HOLIDAYS 2010!

17 Felony Charges: NOT GUILTY

HAPPY NEW YEAR!
PRINCEVILLE PROGRESS REPORT

Contact: 252.823.1057 tel
252.823.5388 fax
www.townofprinceville.org

PRINCEVILLE CONTINUES TO
ASSIST CITIZENS WITH WATER BILL ISSUES,
CONTINUES TO IMPROVE THE TOWN'S FINANCIAL CONDITION, and
WELCOMES A NEW EDGECOMBE COUNTY SOCIAL SERVICES JOBS PROGRAM

Mayor Priscilla Everette-Oates, Town Commissioners, and Town management continue to work overtime on re-shaping and re-focusing the resources of the Town of Princeville. A very special effort continues on bringing a water plant to the Town of Princeville. Mayor Everette-Oates and Team have accomplished this along with many tasks by bringing the town of the "red" into the "black" budget-wise in the first six (6) months of her newly elected term beginning last December 2009.

➢ The Town of Princeville wants any citizen who is having issues or concerns with their water meter reading to contact Ms. Diane Draughn or Town Manager Marrow at 252.823.1057.
Cut-off/Reduced/Written-off Utility Bills Policy
The Town now has a policy that addresses citizen utility bill cut-offs and reduced or written-off utility bills. When emergency circumstances exist on behalf of Town citizens, the Town management can now work out a payment plan with a customer to pay their water and sewer bill over a reasonable period of time.

➢ The Town of Princeville welcomed a new police chief on Monday, December 13, 2010. Please let Chief Joey Petway and his staff know of any safety, security, or police issues at 252.823.1057.

➢ The Princeville Board of Commissioners adopted the *2010-2011 Fiscal Year Budget* and Budget Ordinance. The 2010-2011 Fiscal Year budget is set at **$1,575,122** which represents a decrease in spending of **$368,835** from the 2009-2010 Fiscal Year budget. Therefore, from December 2009 until now, spending has been decreased by $368,835 or 23% of last year's operating budget.

➢ In addition, the North Carolina Department of the State Treasurer has also analyzed the audited financial statements for the Town of Princeville for the year that ended June 30, 2010. The analysis noted that the town has made progress in a number of areas. The NC Department of State Treasurer also noted that audited financial statements were submitted on a timely basis for the second consecutive year, the Town's General Fund balance available increased, and the financial position of the Water and Sewer Fund has improved. The Town's governing board of commissioners, staff, and

PRINCEVILLE PROGRESS REPORT

TOWN OF PRINCEVILLE – PRINCEVILLE, NC

citizens were commended for these improvements. Significant work continues on improving the Town's financial condition and operations. One important change was the Town's negative 0.61% at June 30, 2009 which has increased to a positive 15.85% at the June 30, 2010. Town leadership continues to work on areas of improvement necessary to move Princeville into a solid position of strength.

Town of Princeville and the Edgecombe Department of Social Services

The Town of Princeville and the Edgecombe Department of Social Services have teamed up to offer Princeville citizens the opportunity to apply to the Job Booster grant project underway through the Edgecombe Department of Social Services. The program mirrors the existing Work First initiative and your eligibility will be determined by the Edgecombe Department of Social Services. There is a maximum income and the presence of a school age child in the home requirement for eligibility. **How to Apply:** Applications are taken during the hours of 7:30 a.m. - 5:30 p.m. Monday through Thursday and 7:30 a.m. -5:00 p.m. on Friday for the Tarboro or Rocky Mount Branch offices.

What you will need: Birth Certificates, Social Security Cards, Identification, Previous Months Pay Stubs, Health Insurance Card, Most Recent Bank Statements, Life Insurance Policies, Alien-INS documentation. The names, addresses, date of birth, and social security number of Absent Parent.

North Carolina Foreclosure Prevention FUND- Rocky Mount /Edgecombe Community Development Corporation – 252.212.5830 – www.rmecdc.org

Get Help to Save Your Home. The N. C. Foreclosure Prevention Fund helps North Carolina homeowners who are struggling to pay their mortgage due to job loss or other temporary financial hardship. If you goal is to obtain employment that will allow you to keep you home, it can provide temporary assistance to pay your mortgage while y ou search or train for a new job. The Fund provides assistance at no cost to you.

Am I Eligible?	How Do I Get Help?
You may be eligible for help if you: -are unemployed through no fault of your own or earning less than you have in the past, or -are facing a temporary financial hardship, such as a divorce, serious illness, or the death of a co-signor	-The first step is to make an appointment with a participating, HUD-approved housing counselor who will let you know what documents you need to gather. The counselor will review your situation with you and help you complete an application. -If your lender has already started foreclosure proceedings and you meet preliminary qualifications, the NC Housing Finance Agency may issue a temporary stat-of-foreclosure while you application is under review.
To be eligible, you must also; -need assistance with payments for your principal residence, which must be located in North Carolina, -have satisfactory mortgage payment history prior to your job loss or financial hardship, -demonstrate an ability to resume your mortgage payment once assistance ends, and -be a legal resident of the U.S.	-If you qualify for the loan, the NC Housing Finance Agency will make your mortgage payment directly to your loan provider or bank. At the end of the assistance period, you will resume making your own mortgage payment. -You will pay no interest on your loan, and if you remain in your home for 10 years, your loan will be considered satisfied and you will owe nothing, Your counselor can provide details.

17 Felony Charges: NOT GUILTY

➢ **Whites and Parkers Express Tax Service**

Fast and Accurate
134 Black Street
Princeville, NC 27866
Iris White (252.544.3514)
Shontae White (252.883.1853)

REFUNDS IN A 24-48 HOURS

Refund Direct Deposit
Refund Check
Prepaid Mastercard
Natasha Parker (252) 567.0587 or office (252) 823.8298

➢ Your Money....Your Choice

Once the tax season starts, some tax preparers try to make you think they can get your refund to you faster. What they are offering is a Refund Anticipation Loan (RAL). The loan may sound like a good deal but it is just another way to take your money. (Reprinted from *IRS Remove Debt Indicator for 2011 Tax Filing Season* www.irs.gov on January 4, 2011.)

Get Your Return Prepared Free
Tax Assistance Project 1-800-331-7594
VITA Sites 1-800-829-1040

The Benefit Bank Sites
1-88-756-2463 Ext 244

Prepare Your Own Return with Help
Tax Assistance Project
1-800-331-7594

Prepare Your Own Return Free
www.myfreetaxes.com/legadaidnc
www.thebenefitbank.com

HAPPY NEW YEAR!

➢ *SIMS Metal Management*, the world's largest raw metal recycler, is opening an operation in Princeville and is now taking applications for employment through the Employment Security Commission. People who are interested in this can "register" for SIMS with the Employment Security Commission at:

Edgecombe Community College
2009 West Wilson Street

Tarboro , NC 27886
Office Hours:
Mon - Thu
8:30 AM - 12:00 N
Afternoons by Appointment Only
Phone: 252.823.6742
Jobs Line: 800.768.5627
Fax: 252.641.5799
Email Address: esm.jobs.tarboro@ncesc.gov

PRINCEVILLE PROGRESS REPORT

February 25, 2011

TOWN OF PRINCEVILLE – PRINCEVILLE, NC

HAPPY BIRTHDAY PRINCEVILLE!

PRINCEVILLE PROGRESS REPORT

Contact: 252.823.1057 tel
            252.823.5388 fax
            www.townofprinceville.org

PRINCEVILLE CONTINUES TO
ASSIST CITIZENS WITH WATER BILL ISSUES,
RECENTLY CELEBRATED 126 YEARS OF OPERATIONS AND EXISTENCE, and
Memorialized an original "Buffalo Soldier" Martin Carney

Mayor Priscilla Everette-Oates, Town Commissioners, and Town management continue to work overtime on re-shaping and re-focusing the resources of the Town of Princeville. A very special effort continues on securing funds to bring a water plant to the Town of Princeville. Mayor Everette-Oates and Team have accomplished this along with many tasks by bringing the town of the "red" into the "black" budget-wise in the first six (6) months of her newly elected term beginning December 2009.

HAPPY BIRTHDAY PRINCEVILLE!
"126 Years, That's a long time for anything and we're still Standing Strong"
Princeville Mayor Priscilla Everette-Oates

(Reprint from the Daily Southerner Newspaper) Princeville citizens gathered in the Town Hall, local and state officials came tighter to reflect on Princeville and its place in history. "126 years, that's a long time for anything and we're still standing strong," said Princeville Mayor Priscilla Everette-Oates. Looking back on the history of Princeville through a trivia session was the Princeville Museum and Welcome Center Curator Maggie Boyd. "I will always remember Princeville," she told the crowd. "No matter where I went or who I met, Princeville had my roots.

17 Felony Charges: NOT GUILTY

"We are a people who encourage and invite people to our city," Boyd continued. "You are family when you come here. That's what we're about, making it better for the next generation." Questions were asked about Princeville's past and present, including the year Freedom Hill was founded and who donated the most items to the Princeville Museum and Welcome Center. Prizes were given to those who answered correctly.

On behalf of Gov. Bev Perdue, Angella Dunston, director of the governor's office of citizen and faith outreach, addressed the crowd, asking what Princeville wanted as a birthday gift. "The early residents of this area came together to create a town to symbolize all that we dreamed of," Dunston began. "I want to ask the residents and all of the surrounding counties, what do you want for your birthday? What do you want for your 126th birthday? "Princeville is a gift that freed slaves gave to us 126 years ago," she continued. "This is an example of how people have come together on one accord to pursue a higher goal. Princeville has come a long way and

faced many obstacles. You should continue to celebrate the fact that Princeville is still here and still standing despite all of the change. "The only way we can continue to work together is hand in hand," added Dunston. "I know that you will get what you want when you decide what you want to be your gift."

Assistant Secretary for Community Development Henry McKoy followed Dunston, commenting on the town's longevity and the power of unity. "126 years really is an incredible feat," he said. "If you think about the conditions in which this town was created, this is even more significant. People came out of slavery and were able to come together and found a town. "Who could imagine in 1885 that this community would exist," McKoy continued. "It's communities like this that are most important to our future." McKoy advised Princeville to continue on through the 21st century healthy, wealthy and wise.

Everette-Oates presented Dunston with a plaque for her participation in the Princeville birthday celebration. Dunston accepted on behalf of the Perdue. Milton "The Golden Platter" Bullock led the crowd in a verse of "Happy Birthday" before McKoy cut the first piece of celebratory cake.

SALUTING BUFFALO SOLDIER MARTIN L. CARNEY
(Princeville, North Carolina Native)

The Town of Princeville and its leadership salutes the Martin L. Carney Family. In tribute to the civic and military work of the Mr. Carney, we are grateful for his countless contributions made to the rich history of Princeville. Mr. Carney was 89 and passed on Wednesday, February 16, 2011. Funeral services were held at noon Wednesday at Mayo's Chapel Baptist Church. Burial followed in the Carney Family Cemetery in Princeville.

PRINCEVILLE PROGRESS REPORT

March 25, 2011

TOWN OF PRINCEVILLE – PRINCEVILLE, NC

HAPPY EASTER PRINCEVILLE!
PRINCEVILLE PROGRESS REPORT

Contact: 252.823.1057 tel
            252.823.5388 fax
            www.townofprinceville.org

PRINCEVILLE'S ECONOMIC DEVELOPMENT TEAM WELCOMES PRINCEVILLE CITIZENS TO SIMS METAL MANAGEMENT GRAND OPENING,

CONTINUES TO ASSIST CITIZENS WITH WATER BILL ISSUES, AND RECENTLY CELEBRATED 126 YEARS OF OPERATIONS AND EXISTENCE

Mayor Priscilla Everette-Oates, Town Commissioners, and Town management continue to work overtime on re-shaping and re-focusing the resources of the Town of Princeville. A very special effort continues on securing funds to bring a water plant, water treatment, and drainage system to the Town of Princeville. Mayor Everette-Oates and Team have also accomplished this along with many tasks by bringing the town of the "red" into the "black" budget-wise in the first six (6) months of her newly elected term beginning December 2009.

WELCOME TO PRINCEVILLE SIMS METAL MANAGMENT!

The Town of Princeville in concert with Sims Metal Management is pleased to announce the Grand Opening and Ribbon Cutting of a new metal and electronic recycling company that opens in Princeville, North Carolina next Wednesday, March 30, 2011.
The event is scheduled to commence at 11:00 a.m. and is located at: 1254 U.S. Highway 258 North, Princeville, 27886. The ceremony will be followed by a customer appreciation event. Refreshments will be served.
Town of Princeville citizens should plan to join us at the Customer Appreciation Lunch at 12 Noon.

Join Mayor Priscilla Oates, Town Commissioners, and staff in an official Ribbon Cutting Ceremony.
Sims Metal Management, the world's largest listed metal and electronic recycling company, (www.simsmm.com/US) has announced that its North American Metal Division has opened a facility in Princeville, North Carolina. The recycling facility, named Sims Metal Management – Tar River Recycling, will service the Princeville, Tarboro, Rocky Mount, Greenville and surrounding areas. Sims Metal Management - Tar River Recycling is a 2.5-acre facility located 1254 US 258 North, Princeville NC 27886. The facility will accept all metals, including – but not limited to – iron, steel, copper, brass, aluminum, stainless steel, automobile bodies and will even have car depollution capabilities. Their hours are Monday to Friday, 7:30 AM to 4 PM and Saturday 7 AM to noon, Sims can be reached at (252) 641-4004. he facility also serves the Princeville/Tarboro Area. Sims

17 Felony Charges: NOT GUILTY

PRINCEVILLE PROGRESS REPORT

March 25, 2011

TOWN OF PRINCEVILLE – PRINCEVILLE, NC

Metal Management (www.simsmm.com) is the world's largest listed metal recycler with approximately 240 facilities and 5,700 employees globally. Sims' core businesses are metal recycling and recycling solutions. Sims Metal Management generated approximately 90 percent of its revenue from operations in North America, the United Kingdom, Continental Europe, New Zealand and Asia in fiscal 2010. The Company's ordinary shares are listed on the Australian Securities Exchange (ASX: SGM) and its ADRs are listed on the New York Stock Exchange (NYSE: SMS).

Website: www.simsmm.com/US

➢ The Town of Princeville wants any citizen who is having issues or concerns with their water meter reading to contact Ms. Diane Draughn or Town Manager Marrow at 252.823.1057.
Cut-off/Reduced/Written-off Utility Bills Policy
The Town now has a policy that addresses citizen utility bill cut-offs and reduced or written-off utility bills. When emergency circumstances exist on behalf of Town citizens, the Town management can now work out a payment plan with a customer to pay their water and sewer bill over a reasonable period of time.

➢ **North Carolina Foreclosure Prevention FUND- Rocky Mount /Edgecombe Community Development Corporation – 252.212.5830 – www.rmecdc.org**
Get Help to Save Your Home. The N. C. Foreclosure Prevention Fund helps North Carolina homeowners who are struggling to pay their mortgage due to job loss or other temporary financial hardship. If you goal is to obtain employment that will allow you to keep you home, it can provide temporary assistance to pay your mortgage while you search or train for a new job. The Fund provides assistance at no cost to you.

Am I Eligible?	How Do I Get Help?
You may be eligible for help if you: -are unemployed through no fault of your own or earning less than you have in the past, or -are facing a temporary financial hardship, such as a divorce, serious illness, or the death of a co-signor	-The first step is to make an appointment with a participating, HUD-approved housing counselor who will let you know what documents you need to gather. The counselor will review your situation with you and help you complete an application. -If your lender has already started foreclosure proceedings and you meet preliminary qualifications, the NC Housing Finance Agency may issue a temporary stat-of-foreclosure while you application is under review.
To be eligible, you must also: -need assistance with payments for your principal residence, which must be located in North Carolina, -have satisfactory mortgage payment history prior to your job loss or financial hardship, -demonstrate an ability to resume your mortgage payment once assistance ends, and -be a legal resident of the U.S.	-If you qualify for the loan, the NC Housing Finance Agency will make your mortgage payment directly to your loan provider or bank. At the end of the assistance period, you will resume making your own mortgage payment. -You will pay no interest on your loan, and if you remain in your home for 10 years, your loan will be considered satisfied and you will owe nothing, Your counselor can provide details.

42

The following pages show various community events for residents of Princeville, planned by the Economic Development Committee.

The Daily Southerner, Tarboro, NC

November 15, 2011

Department of Transportation Business Developer Specialist Eric Miller, DOT, Workforce Development Manager, Marvin T. Butler, Princeville Mayor Priscilla Everette-Oates and DOT Small Business Enterprise Coordinator Thomas Burt attended Princeville Job Employment and Career Day Expo Wednesday at the town hall. Approximately 40 people attended the event. Photo/Calvin Adkins

News Story

Princeville to host 'Survivor Week'

Sports Editor
Calvin Adkins

TARBORO — PRINCEVILLE — Twelve years have passed since Hurricane Floyd's floodwater devastated the town of Princeville. Princeville leaders are making sure that no one forgets it.

In an effort to "celebrate the recovery," the the town is sponsoring "Princeville Survivor Week."

"We're doing this because we shouldn't forget where we came from," said Everette Oates, who was referring to Hurricane Floyd flood water that devastated Princeville in September 1999. "

The event will kickoff on Wednesday with Jobs Employment and Career Day Expo at the Town Hall.

From 10 a.m. to 3 p.m. the N.C. Department of Transportation will accept applications. DOT officials will also allow potential applicants to sit in on an on-the-job training and pre-employment training sessions. A network session is scheduled for 3:30 p.m. to 5 p.m.

424

17 Felony Charges: NOT GUILTY

Following Wednesday's job expo, the the town will sponsor a Resource Training Summit from 8:45 a.m. to 4 p.m. Thursday and Friday on the Tarboro Campus of the Edgecombe Community College inside the Thomas Fleming Building. Several workshops will be held throughout the day and state and local speakers will address the crowd.

Joyce Mitchell, state community outreach director for the office of U.S. Senator, will be the speaker for Thursday's morning event and Dr. Alma C. Hobbs, the associate assistant secretary for administration for the United States Department of Agriculture, is the keynote speaker for the planned luncheon.

On Friday, Henry McKoy, assistant secretary for Commerce for the N.C. Department of Commerce in Raleigh is the morning speaker and Andrea Harris, president of the N.C. Institute of Minority, Economic Development of Durham will be the keynote speaker.

Princeville Mayor Priscilla Everette-Oates said the dignitaries will discuss matters pertaining to grants along with other matters that can help improve municipalities.

Registration fee for the two-day event is $100 for elected officials and $75 for their guests. Registration fee for a citizen is $50.

"We're linking the local, state and the federal agencies together to bring resources to this area," Everette-Oates said. "This is not just for Princeville, it's for everybody. We're asking for leaders from all over the county and outside the county to come and help make this event successful."

Priscilla E. Oates

PRINCEVILLE SURVIVOR WEEK

SEPTEMBER 12-17, 2011
PRINCEVILLE, NC

17 Felony Charges: NOT GUILTY

PRINCEVILLE SURVIVOR WEEK

Day	September 12-17, 2011	Event Title, Location, Details
1	Monday, September 12, 2011 4:00-10:00 pm	*Princeville FESTIVAL* Downtown Princeville, NC – Riverside Heritage Park Admission: TBA
2	Tuesday, September 13, 2011 4:00-10:00 pm	*Princeville FESTIVAL* Downtown Princeville, NC – Riverside Heritage Park Admission: TBA
3	Wednesday, September 14, 2011 *Workshops* 10:00 am – 3:00 pm	*Princeville Jobs, Employment, and Career Day* Town of Princeville Town Hall Building 201 Main Street – Princeville, NC 27886 Admission: FREE
	Networking Reception 3:30-5:00 pm	*Princeville Jobs, Employment, and Career Day* *Networking Reception* Town of Princeville Town Hall Building 201 Main Street – Princeville, NC 27886 - Admission: FREE
	Princeville FESTIVAL 4:00-10:00 pm	*Princeville FESTIVAL* Downtown Princeville, NC – Riverside Heritage Park Admission: TBA
4	Thursday, September 15, 2011 *Workshops* 8:45-12 Noon & 1:30-4:00 pm	*Princeville Town Resources Training Summit* *Linking the Local, State, and National (Federal)* Thomas S. Fleming Building, Mobley Atrium Edgecombe Community College, Tarboro Campus 2009 West Wilson Street- Tarboro, NC 27886
	Luncheon 12 Noon – 1:30 pm	*Resources Training Summit LUNCHEON* ECC, Tarboro Campus, Mobley Atrium 2009 West Wilson Street- Tarboro, NC 27886
	Princeville FESTIVAL 4:00-10:00 pm	*Princeville FESTIVAL* Downtown Princeville, NC – Riverside Heritage Park - Admission:
5	Friday, September 16, 2011 *Workshops* 8:45-12 Noon &	*Princeville Town Resources Training Summit* *Linking the Local, State, and National (Federal)* Thomas S. Fleming Building, Mobley Atrium Edgecombe Community College, Tarboro Campus 2009 West Wilson Street- Tarboro, NC 27886
	Luncheon 12 Noon – 2:00 pm	PRINCEVILLE SURVIVOR DAY *LUNCHEON* ECC, Tarboro Campus, Mobley Atrium 2009 West Wilson Street- Tarboro, NC 27886
	4:00-11:00 pm	*Princeville FESTIVAL* Downtown Princeville, NC – Riverside Heritage Park Admission: TBA
6	Saturday, September 13, 2011 12:00-11:00 pm	*Princeville FESTIVAL* Downtown Princeville, NC – Riverside Heritage Park Admission: TBA

409

46

Priscilla E. Oates

PRINCEVILLE SURVIVOR WEEK
Princeville Town Resources Training Summit
Linking the Local, State, and National (Federal)
Town Resources Training Summit

REGISTRATION FORM

NAME	
ADDRESS	
CITY, STATE, ZIP	
EMAIL ADDRESS	
TELEPHONE (Work & Cell)	
FAX	
CHECKS PAYABLE TO:	Town of Princeville – *Survivor Day 2011*.
CHECKS MAILED TO:	Town of Princeville, 201 South Main Street, Princeville, NC 27886 Attn: Ms. Diana Draughn, Princeville Finance Director Address Finance Questions at: 252.823.1057

SUMMIT REGISTRATION CHOICES

Quantity	Cost	Type of Registration	Sub-Total	Grand Total
	$100	SUMMIT REGISTRATION – Elected Officials		
	$ 75	SUMMIT REGISTRATION – Summit Guests		
	$50	SUMMIT REGISTRATION – Citizens *****		
	$100	FULL PAGE AD		
	$ 50	½ PAGE AD		
	$ 25	¾ PAGE AD		
	$ 50	VENDOR / BOOTH REGISTRATION		
TOTAL	----------	GRAND TOTAL OF REGISTRATION CHOICES	----------------	Grand Total

FURTHER QUESTIONS PERTAINING TO SUMMIT REGISTRATION MAY BE ADDRESSED TO pprincevillenc@gmail.com OR TO REQUEST AN ELECTRONIC REGISTRATION FORM.

***** -Some Sponsorship dollars may be used to offset cost of *Citizens Registration* to the Summit.

410

47

Princeville Survivor Week 2011
Hotel Accommodations

Best Western Tarboro Hotel

102 Market Center Drive
Tarboro, North Carolina 27886
800.937.8376 Tel
252.824.0362 Fax
www.bestwestern.com

Hotel Amenities
Free Breakfast Bar
High Speed Internet Access
Fitness Center
Outdoor Pool

GROUP BLOCK OF ROOMS

Name: Princeville Survivor Week 2011

Type of Rooms: Doubles and Kings

Rate: $62.00 plus tax ($4.19)

Total: $66.19

Call 252.824.0700

Reserve Your Accommodations by

September 9, 2011

Princeville Survivor Week 2011
Hotel Accommodations

Comfort Inn Hotel

1504 Western Blvd.
Tarboro, North Carolina 27886
252.824.0088 Tel
252.824.0090 Fax
www.comfortinn.com

Hotel Amenities
Fitness Center
High Speed Internet Access
Meeting Space
Outdoor Pool

GROUP BLOCK OF ROOMS

Name: Princeville Survivor Week 2011

Type of Rooms: Doubles and Kings

Rate: $63.00 plus tax ($4.25)

Total: $67.25

Call 252.824.0088

Reserve Your Accommodations by

September 9, 2011

Wallace Green was a commercial real estate broker who assisted my administration and the Economic Development Committee with researching prospective land, buildings and businesses to bring to Princeville. The following pages are emails and notes to further demonstrate the validity and purpose of the Economic Development Committee.

PRINCEVILLE ECONOMIC DEVELOPMENT PROJECTS

TO: Mayor Priscilla Everett-Oates
           Victor Marrow
FROM: Wallace Green (919.630.0180)

DATE: June 29, 2011

PROJECT	Objectives and Status
306 Mutual Boulevard Deed Book 1151 Page 250	• Property has been listed for sale with Coldwell Banker Commercial TradeMark Properties (Wallace Green) • Objective is sale to a retail business, including fast food, grocery, or a financial institution. • A small grocery store chain may be interested in the site if a 10,000 sq.ft. building can be constructed. Discussion is needed asap re sources of funding for site work and building construction. (see below re 308 Mutual)
308 Mutual Boulevard	• Acquistion of 308 Mutual is critical to attracting a retail business. Together with 306 Mutual, the properties will total 1.56 acres, approximately the same size as the Dollar General property, which is 1.33 acres. • The house on the property must be relocated • The Town is working on this.
Relocation of Fire Department	• Town is working on this.

Princeville Business Park	• Coldwell Banker TMP is focused on contacting all property owners along Ridgewood Road, from Commercial Road to State Highway 33 to participate in a marketing program to attract new investment and jobs to Princeville.
	• The Town should place contact all property owners in this area inviting to allow the Town to designate the area as Princeville Business Park. The Town should pay for 2 large signs on the property "Princeville Business Park" and the Coldwell Banker TMP phone number. The signs should be visible from Hwy 64. CB can assist with the design.
	• Properties now listed for Sale by CB:
	   1. The former truck stop
	   2.
	   3.

Princeville BioEnergy Project	• Secure a commitment from the Edgecombe- Martin County EMC to purchase renewable energy from a bio-energy system that would be designed and constructed for the Town • The Town Manager is arranging a preliminary meeting to be attended by Wallace Green who has identified a technology provider to design and construct the system. • The Town will need to raise the necessary funds for construction and operation of the system. The budget will depend upon the agreement with the EMC.
Feasibility of Town owned Waste and Drinking Water Treatment utility	• A private equity fund has expressed interest in conducting a feasibility study. Information regarding the fund is located at the following web site, and the Mayor is advised to consult with the Town attorney about how best to proceed with an initial discussion about the potential approach. www.AmericanInfrastructureInvestors.com NOTE: The result of this type of transaction would mean that the system is designed, built, and operated by the investor. Financial benefits to the Town would be negotiated, thus the need to discuss this with the Town attorney.
Grant Writing	The following grants are being prepared at your request: {{TABLE}}

The following grants are being prepared at your request:

Grantor&Writer	Purpose/Status	Due Date
EPA	Brownfields Assessment re Ridgewood site, and Mutual Blvd. site; Waiting on call from Atlanta office	TBD

Priscilla E. Oates

From: wgreen@cbctmp.com [mailto:wgreen@cbctmp.com]
To: victormarrow@townofprinceville.org
Cc: dtawwab@gmail.com
Sent: Tue, 7 Feb 2012 18:48:07 -0500
Subject: Princeville Economic Development

Victor -- received your message and a call from the Mayor. Please share this with her as she may have been inquiring about the same items:

1. Marketing of Business Park -- as you may have noticed, we have some of the Ridgewood properties for sale and are working on others. I sent the budget for the sign and the design earlier. We need to talk about how to contract with the sign company and who will do the installation. Perhaps your maintenance staff can handle that. We will identify the location of each sign. One at either end of Ridgewood.

2. Marketing of the Diggs and Wiggins properties -- it took quite a while but this week I have confirmed with both of them their intent to sell and I hope to have them sign listing agreements when I come over for the environmental assessment meeting at Ridgewood later this month.

3. Mutual Boulevard -- I am concerned about the offer we received on the Mutual site and that the Town never responded. What is the status of securing the adjacent lot? We cannot do much marketing until the Town owns the site. I think the grocery store and restaurant ideas are feasible if we can build the building. However, I do not want to spend any time on it until the Town owns the entire parcel. The Commerce Department, Rural Center, and Golden Leaf could be sources of funding.

17 Felony Charges: NOT GUILTY

In addition, I am hoping to meet with the County Manager at some point after we get the business park signs up to ask for help by placing the project site on the County and the State Department of Commerce web sites.

Finally, it would be good if you could also find about $10,000 or something close to it so that we could contract with NC Connected to upgrade the Town web site so that the good things you are doing are better displayed, and so that local real estate investment opportunities can receive broader distribution.

Wallace O. Green
Commercial Real Estate Broker
Director, Public Private Partnerships
919.630.0180

Priscilla E. Oates

From:	Wallace Green (Wallace.Green@rada-nc.com)	Date:	Sun, 17 Jul 2011 23:28:54 -0400
To:	mayoroates@townofprinceville.org		
Subject:	Banks - SBA Lenders		

Mayor – the following banks are actively pursuing SBA loans. I recommend you begin with the first one, as I recently met with Dave White at Bank of NC.

1. Bank of North Carolina – Dave White; 919.232.6828: www.bankofnc.com
2. Capital Bank – Kelly Ferrante; www.capitalbank-nc.com
3. Fifth Third Bank – www.53.com

Wallace

Wallace O. Green
President
Raleigh Area Development Authority
4030 Wake Forest Road - Suite 205
Raleigh, NC 27609
www.rada-nc.com
919.807.8400

From:	Wallace Green (Wallace.Green@rada-nc.com)	Date:	Thu, 7 Jul 2011 18:56:08 -0400
To:	mayoroates@townofprinceville.org, victormarrow@townofprinceville.org		
Cc:	Wallace Green, wgreen@cbctmp.com		
Subject:	Grocery Store Interest in Mutual Boulevard Location		

Mayor Oates, I spoke with an owner of a small local chain of grocery stores here in Raleigh and he is interested in the Mutual Boulevard location. In order to pursue this, we need to accomplish the following:

1. Secure ownership of the adjacent lot which will provide a total of approximately 1 acre. I can pursue this if you put me in touch with the appropriate persons.
2. Secure funds to construct a 10,000 – 15,000 sq ft building for the food store; the food store will need to sign a lease sufficient to cover a portion of the building cost.
3. Determine from the NC Rural Center if the Building Re-Use program will be available to cover a portion of the building cost; this is a matching grant program; the balance would be covered by a loan from either Rural Center, Golden Leaf, Commerce, or Department of Agriculture. I have placed a call to the Rural Center to find out if Building Re-Use funds are available to relocate a vacant building to the site.
4. The grocery chain operates a 30,000 sq ft store in West Raleigh which you can visit when you come. However, we should resolve item #1 first.

Wallace

Wallace O. Green
President
Raleigh Area Development Authority
4030 Wake Forest Road - Suite 205
Raleigh, NC 27609
www.rada-nc.com
919.807.8400

17 Felony Charges: NOT GUILTY

From: wgreen@cbctmp.com
To: mayoroates@townofprinceville.org
Cc: wgreen@cbctmp.com
Subject: CONFIDENTIAL - Fast Food Restaurant Prospects

Date: Fri, 8 Jul 2011 16:35:59 -0400

Here is the list of prospects we are pursuing. Others will be added. Please keep confidential until we have a commitment. I will let you know when a call from you would be helpful:

Fast Food With Seating and Drive Thru Stores:

- Hardee's - under consideration
- Andy's - Waiting on call back
- Popeye's - No Interest/Tarboro Store
- BoJangles - Spoke with headquarters; Now waiting on call from regional franchisee
- Biscuitville - No Interest
- Chick Fil'A - Spoke with headquarters in Atlanta; waiting for next call.
- Subway - May look at small space rental in larger strip center
- TacoBell - Spoke with headquarters; will follow up next week
- Zaxby's - Waiting on call back
- Checkers - Waiting on call back
- Papa Johns Pizza - no contact yet
- CiCi's Pizza - no contact yet
- Dominos Pizza - no contact yet
- GodFather's Pizza - may consider rent of small space
- Pizza Hut - no contact

Wallace O. Green
Commercial Real Estate Broker
Director, Public Private Partnerships
919.630.0180

The Daily Southerner, Tarboro, NC

November 18, 2011

Princeville Mayor Priscilla Everette-Oates, left, give gratitude to Dr. Alma Hobbs, associated assistant secretary for administration for the United States Department of Agriculture, Thursday during Princeville's Resource Training Summit on the campus of Edgecombe Community College inside the Mobley Atrium. The summit will kicked off again 8:45 a.m. today_____ Photo/Calvin Adkins

News Story

Federal officials are aware of Princeville's need for a water tower

Sports Editor
Calvin Adkins

TARBORO — A representative of the federal government gave Princeville a glimmer of hope of receiving an item that is desperately on the town's wish list Thursday during the second day of 'Princeville Survivor Week' at Edgecombe Community College in the Mobley Atrium of the Thomas Fleming Building.

"I leave you to ponder, what can you do to help and more important what can you do to help Mayor (Priscilla Everette-)Oates in obtaining a water plant for the citizens of Princeville?" said Dr. Alma Hobbs, associate assistant secretary for administration for the United States Department of Agriculture. "This is the question, and the answer lies in those hearing the question."

Although Hobb's remark did not earmark any money for the project, it served notice that federal officials are aware of Princeville's cry for a water plant. Her remark received an arousing applause from the approximately 75 people attending the noon luncheon event.

After the noon luncheon, Randall Gore, director of N.C. Rural Development and Dennis Patton,

419

55

17 Felony Charges: NOT GUILTY

director of planning and development services for Upper Coastal Plain Council of Government conducted workshops.

The purpose of the two-day event is to "link local, state and national resources and services."

Throughout the week, Everette-Oates reiterated that the invited government officials could be links to projects for Princeville and other municipalities in the surrounding area.

One of the biggest projects that Princeville is pursuing is a water treatment

plant in hopes of aiding its citizens and potentially reducing the seemingly astronomical monthly water and sewer bills that they currently pay. Princeville buys its water from the adjacent town, Tarboro.

"Our main focus is to get a water plant to reduce the cost of water for our citizens," Everette-Oates said. "We need resources to get it done and that's why we invited these people to come today. They're not here for just Princeville, but for the entire Edgecombe County."

Hobbs said, "Together, there is hope in knowing that we have the expertise, the resources to make the difference that needs to be made. So get to know your state, local and national partners. They are——here to help you."

Around noon, the sparse crowd began to populate with students from the college as well as a few Princeville citizens.

The event was the first day for the Town Resources Training Summit. Today, the summit is scheduled to kickoff again at 8:45 a.m. with the morning speaker, Henry McKoy, assistant secretary for commerce, and the luncheon speaker, Andrea Harris, president of N.C. Institute of Minority. To attend the two-day event, elected officials were charged $100 and Princeville citizens $50. On Wednesday that fee was waived and attendees, including students from the college who were given an invitation, attended the luncheon for free.

The Daily Southerner, Tarboro, NC

November 21, 2011

Andrea Harris, president of the N.C. Institute of Minority, speaks to an audience Friday during the second day of Princeville Town Resources Training Summit on the campus of Edgecombe Community College inside the Mobley Atrium. More than 100 people attended the luncheon. Photo/Calvin Adkins

News Story

Survival Day 2: 'Princeville has come a long ways'

Sports Editor
Calvin Adkins

TARBORO — "You all have come a long way."

Those were some of the encouraging remarks offered to Princeville citizens by Andrea Harris, president of the N.C. Institute of Minority Friday during the second day of Princeville's Town Resources Training Summit on the campus of Edgecombe Community College inside the Mobley Atrium. The event was the third day of Princeville Survivor Week Celebration.

Harris has worked with Princeville on several projects since 1995. The organization she was working with back then had sketched the renovation for the historic town hall. Before the project came to fruition, Hurricane Floyd floodwaters wreaked havoc on the entire town.

When it was time to rebuild, the town opted to build a new town hall on Main Street and restore the old town hall and use it as a museum.

17 Felony Charges: NOT GUILTY

Harris recalled the town hall meetings when the elected officials voted 3-2 to keep its charter. Soon after in another meeting, an official from the Army Corps of Engineers suggested that the town should not rebuild.

"I just couldn't understand how this man could sit there and tell everybody in Princeville they were not going to rebuild the dike," Harris said. "They were going to level the town. I got beyond myself. I said, 'You going to sit here and the people told you what they wanted to do and you going to tell them you are going to level their town? When I think about that, I celebrate you."

Today, Princeville's population is back to more than 2,000 citizens. The majority of the businesses rebuilt and new homes are strewn throughout the town.

Princeville Mayor Priscilla Everette-Oates, who organized the town's first Survival Day during her first administration, was ecstatic about the event.

"It is important that we don't forget what happened to us on Sept. 16. (1999) she said. "We're going to do this annually."

During the first day of "Survival Week" the town organized the Job Employment and Career Day Expo with the Department of Transportation as the facilitators. Approximately 45 people attended the expo.

The town kicked off the second day with the training summit at Edgecombe Community College. The noon keynote speaker was Dr. Alma Hobbs, Associated Assistant Secretary for Administration for the United States Department of Agriculture in Washington D.C. Several workshops concerning resources for municipalities were held.

Friday's session drew the largest crowd with approximately 100 people attending the noon luncheon.

"Princeville has come a long way and they have done great job rebuilding the town and I'm sure there are better things to come," Harris said. "I'm glad to be a part of this celebration. It means a lot to me. After going through these workshops, you will leave here better off than you were in the past."

The summit was advertised to cost $100 for elected officials and $50 for Princeville citizens. Those fees were waived by Everett-Oates after "someone donated money to pay for the food." she said.

"When I think about Princeville I think about the fact that you got history of a people who was not afraid to walk across the Tar River and create a town after the civil war. That took all kinds of courage. It took a whole different type of courage."

"You said I'm going to create my own space I'm going to create my own neighbor hood. You still have a neighbor hood. You ought to celebrate it."

Princeville has come a long way and they have done great job rebuilding the town and I'm sure there are better things to come, Harris added. To be a part of this celebration means a lot to me."

First time I came here and every time I come here I feel closure to me my own self. Because you

422

reminds me of myself just because your will to survive your will to live. That might be a small thing for you because you are so comfortable to that. You are comfortable to people coming in and celebrating and all that. you know more about the things. you know the good the bad and ugly and all of the rest of. I'm going to tell you what all the rest of us think sometimes. Because sometimes it takes someone from the outside to make that can tell you all of the things that you can celebrate.

rebuilding the town and I'm sure there are better things to come. be a part of this celebration means a lot to me. Workshop knowing that when you leave here you will be better off than you were in the future.

"Every time I come to Princeville there is a poem I think of and it says

If there any place you can go and understand and see the determination of people, it is Princeville."

"You are faith. Faith is the Hope in believing despite of the evidence. Look at you today. It may not be all that you want it to be. It surely is not what it was." Harris stated.

Princeville Thanks Durham

Mayor Priscilla Everette-Oates (left)Pro-Tem Isabelle Purvis-Andrews(middle) and Town Manager Victor Morrow (back right)

presented a plaque of appreciation to

Mayor William Bell (holding plaque) & members of Durham City Council for their donation of the 5 vehicles to Princeville.

339

60

Below are the 5 vehicles donated to the town of
Princeville by Mayor William Bell of Durham, NC in 2003

DURHAM CITY GOVERNMENT VEHICLE DONATIONS

3 POLICE CRUISERS

1 TRASH TRUCK

1 DUMP TRUCK

PRINCEVILLE MAYOR
PRISCILLA E. OATES
TOWN OF PRINCEVILLE

DURHAM MAYOR
WILLIAM V. BELL
CITY OF DURHAM

**TOWN OF PRINCEVILLE THANKS THE
CITY OF DURHAM FOR VEHICLES**

17 Felony Charges: NOT GUILTY

Mayor Priscilla Everette-Oates and local officials attended Princeville's Dollar General's ribbon cutting on May 29, 2010 Richard Overton, District Manager, stated that sales at Princeville's Dollar General Store were more than the two Dollar General Stores in Tarboro and the surrounding stores.

Dr. Joseph Lowery

THE DAILY SOUTHERNER
Monday, February 15, 2005

Happy 120ᵗʰ Birthday, Princeville

On Friday, February 18, 2005, the Town of Princeville will celebrate its 120th birthday. Starting time is 12:00 noon. It will be held at the Saint Luke Church of Christ located at 101 Neville Street in Princeville, NC. The keynote speaker will be the Dr. Joseph Lowery of the Southern Christian Leadership Conference (SCLC). Dr. Lowery is the co-founder of the SCLC with the late Dr. Martin Luther King, Jr.

Refreshments will be served immediately after the celebration.
The public is invited to attend.

For further information, please call (252) 823-1057 and someone will assist you.

Rocky Mount Telegram
Saturday, February 19, 2005

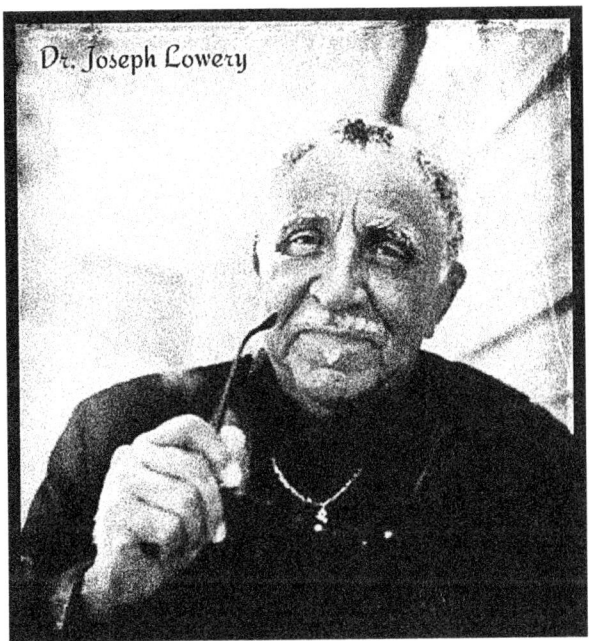

Dr. Joseph Lowery

Princeville celebrates its 120th birthday

By NATALIE JORDAN
Staff Writer

PRINCEVILLE – As a church in a small town began to fill, a father and son took their seats, ready for what was in store.

Gregory Horne and his 6-year-old son Joshua Whitehead sat waiting Friday like everyone else inside St. Luke Church of Christ in Princeville – the oldest American town chartered by blacks that was settled in 1865 and incorporated in 1885. But this wasn't an ordinary church service.

As the town gathered to celebrate 120 years of history for its birthday, they also gathered to hear the Rev. Dr. Joseph Lowery – one of the original founders of the Southern Christian Leadership Conference – as a birthday gift.

"I came out to support Princeville and to take part in the celebration, and see Rev. Lowery," said Horne of Tarboro. "I think this is a historical event. Whoever thought of the idea deserves a lot of credit."

Playing with his father's hands, Joshua said, "I'm excited. This is history, and I'm part of it."

Though Joshua didn't stay awake to hear Lowery, the boy was part of another moment in Princeville's recorded events.

After singing the national Negro

783

See BIRTHDAY, 2A

63

17 Felony Charges: NOT GUILTY

<u>News Release...February 16, 2012</u>
Happy Birthday PRINCEVILLE!
... 127 Years Later ...

CELEBRATION KEYNOTE and BIRTHDAY RECEPTION
Town of Princeville 127th Birthday Celebration
Saturday, February 25, 2012 – 10:00 A.M.
Princeville Town Hall Building
201 South Main Street – Princeville, North Carolina 27886
252.823.1057 Telephone

Mayor Priscilla Everette-Oates and the Town of Princeville, North Carolina will celebrate 127 years of existence and operations. This amounts to the 127th birthday year. A reception that includes birthday cake will follow the celebration keynote. This event continues to create links to hopes, dreams, and the future of Princeville.

Congressman G. K. Butterfield is a lifelong resident of Wilson, N.C., and has served the people of the First Congressional District of North Carolina since 2004. His father was a well-respected dentist and elected official in Wilson, N.C., and his mother was a classroom teacher for 48 years.

Congressman Butterfield graduated from Charles H. Darden High School before earning a Bachelor of Arts degree from North Carolina Central University (NCCU), in Durham, North Carolina. He later earned a Juris Doctorate degree from NCCU School of Law.

For 14 years, Congressman Butterfield practiced law in his home community, and was best known for his success with several eastern North Carolina voting rights lawsuits that resulted in African-American communities having the ability to elect candidates of their choice to public office.

In 1988, Congressman Butterfield was elected Resident Superior Court Judge for the First Judicial Division. For the next 12 years, he presided over civil and criminal court in 46 counties of North Carolina.

In February 2001, then-Judge Butterfield was appointed to the North Carolina Supreme Court but was defeated in the November 2002 election. After his defeat, he was then appointed to the Superior Court bench to resume his duties as a trial judge.

After serving 15 years as a state judge, in 2004, Congressman Butterfield retired after being selected as the Democratic nominee in the special election to fill the unexpired term as U.S. Representative for North Carolina's First Congressional District. He was first elected on July 20, 2004, and continues to serve today.

787

{ 1 }

64

In the 110th Congress, Congressman Butterfield became part of House leadership with an appointment as a Chief Deputy Whip. Chief Deputy Whips are responsible for helping to formulate policy and for ensuring the passage of legislation. He is the first Democrat from North Carolina to serve as a Chief Deputy Whip.

Congressman Butterfield serves on the powerful House Committee on Energy and Commerce. He serves as the Ranking Democrat on the Subcommittee on Commerce, Manufacturing and Trade. The subcommittee's jurisdiction includes interstate and foreign commerce, including all trade matters within the jurisdiction of the full committee; regulation of commercial practices, including sports-related matters; consumer affairs, consumer protection, consumer product safety and product liability; motor vehicle safety; and regulation of travel and tourism.

Congressman Butterfield previously served as vice chairman of the Energy Subcommittee in the 111th Congress and now serves as a member of the Subcommittee on Environment and the Economy.

Congressman Butterfield is an honorably discharged veteran of the U.S. Army. His family includes adult daughters Valeisha, Lenai and Tunya; and son-in-law, Dahntay.

#########

About the Town of Princeville

Princeville, North Carolina is the oldest incorporated Black town in the United States. It is located in the Coastal Plain region of eastern North Carolina and lies just south of the Tar River from the county seat of Tarboro in Edgecombe County. Settled just after the Civil War in 1865, Princeville was originally called "Freedom Hill" by the freed slaves who had gathered on this Tar River flood plain seeking refuge at a Union Army camp that was located there. Throughout its history, Princeville has endured racial intimidation, economic and social isolation, and repeated flooding (e.g. 1800, 1865, 1889, 1919, 1924, 1940, and 1958), but it has steadfastly persisted as a cohesive, African-American community.

After the building of a levee in 1965 to prevent major flooding, the town saw many modern improvements, the expanding of its borders, a growth in population and an increase in the number of businesses. In 1999 a 500-year flood caused by Hurricanes Dennis and Floyd broke the levee and wiped out the town, bringing national attention to the historical and social significance of Princeville as a symbol of African American perseverance and self determination. Today this 98% African American town of approximately 2,100 people is rapidly rebuilding from the devastation of the flood of 1999 and is very proud of its unique place within African American heritage and United States history. This unique sense of place and solidarity among Princeville's town members, along with the destruction of physical historical documents from the flooding of its past, make it an ideal community in which to begin the preservation of oral history.

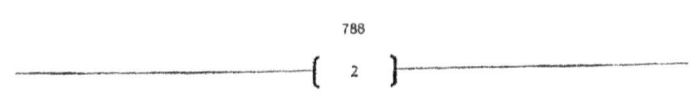

HAPPY BIRTHDAY
TOWN OF PRINCEVILLE
127 YEARS!!

KEYNOTE SPEAKER

THE HONORABLE G. K. BUTTERFIELD
UNITED STATES CONGRESSMAN FIRST
CONGRESSIONAL DISTRICT
STATE OF NORTH CAROLINA

SATURDAY, FEBRUARY 25, 2012 - 10:00 AM

PRINCEVILLE TOWN HALL BUILDING
201 EAST MAIN STREET
PRINCEVILLE, N.C. 27886

3.

Attorney Charles Bonner

After I had been indicted, I got a call from my lawyer. We were at the auditor's house who I hired in 2002 and we got the phone call that they were going to indict me.

I had to get back home and I couldn't believe it. I had to stand in front of the judge and the people I usually help out. Here I am seeing people in the court who I helped out and now I had to go in front of the judge to be indicted. Each charge was 4 ½ years and there were 17 charges. Again, they were trying to send me to prison for 75 years for something I didn't do!

After that, they gave a plea bargain and I wouldn't take it. The bargain was for me to accept 3 of the 17 charges and I would not be able to sign any more checks; not even checks for my own company.

I told one of my NC lawyers I was not signing it because I did not do anything and the LGC and the state auditor are afraid of what may come up with them doing the stealing. Not me. I was not taking those charges.

They told me I may want to take it because at least I wouldn't be going to prison. I said I wasn't going to prison and I wasn't accepting the plea bargain. I stood firm that I did not do it. It would be seen in the end they were the ones hiding the town of Princeville's information; taking documents from the town manager and she told me how the

LGC took files from the campus without her permission. They finally got rid of all the Princeville staff and most of the police officers except for one or two.

I refused to take any plea bargains.

One of my NC lawyers thought taking the plea bargain would be the best thing for me to do and I said no. I told him he would see how they were taking the documents, concealing them, then they wrote a report like I never turned in receipts from credit cards that were used for the town of Princeville.

That's when I called Atty Bonner. I was crying and I told him I had to get someone outside of NC so there would be no connection. It was critical at this point that I had legal representation that had no connection to NC head officials that I was dealing with.

God truly blessed me with Atty Bonner. He was a civil rights lawyer from Sausalito, California and we met in January 2014 to get started immediately on the investigation. He literally wasted no time! He and his legal Dream Team came in like blood hounds ready to sniff out evidence and find their target! They conducted depositions, interviews, in-depth investigations and more. I was excited seeing all of these things taking place because for the very first time, someone believed me entirely! Atty Bonner was on my side and he truly believed everything I was telling him about my innocence.

I had another trial date and he filed a motion advising I had a new lawyer. Filing that motion caused the trial date to be pushed back. He was able to secure two additional lawyers, Ryan Stump and Samuel Randall, from a law firm in Charlotte, NC as he had to be sworn in to North Carolina in order to practice there as he was not a resident of NC and not part of the NC bar.

During the investigation, Atty Bonner wrote an 8-page demand letter to SBI and SBI Agent Lolita Chapman to immediately stop badgering and bullying my clients at my businesses while trying to find fault with me and my administration. He listed specific complaints from them that talked about how Agent Chapman was rude, did not show her ID badge and she was very intimidating.

LAW OFFICES OF CHARLES A. BONNER
475 Gate 5 Road, Suite 212
Sausalito, CA 94965
Tel: (415) 331-3070
Fax: (415) 331-2738

February 28, 2014

State Bureau of Investigation
North Carolina Department of Justice
SBI Agent Lolita B. Chapman
SBI Agent John Taylor
1013 W. H. Smith Blvd.
Greenville, NC 27834
(919) 662-4500

A Bill of Rights is what the people are entitled to against every government,
and what no just government should refuse, or rest on inference. Thomas Jefferson

Re: Notice and Demand per 42 U.S.C. §§ 1983, 1986, 1985; 18 USC §242, 18 USC §245

Ms. Chapman and Mr. Taylor:

Please be informed that our office has been retained by and represents Ex-Mayor Priscilla Everette-Oates, resident of Princeville, NC.

Statement of Facts:

Recently we were consulted by several African-American individuals whom you interrogated regarding Mayor Oates. Some of these individuals are elderly and infirm, suffering illnesses, and some are clients of D-Pom, a community service center owned and operated by Ex-Mayor Priscilla Oates and her husband, the Reverend Duarthur Oates. D-Pom provides a variety of social services to an economically depressed class of people, including mental illness counseling, drug counseling, and educational classes, including university affiliated program preparing and teaching clients to obtain GED certification. Mayor and Pastor Oates also operate a food bank, providing free food for the hungry, which they have successfully operated continuously for more than 10 years.

Each of the individuals who complained to us about your coercive conduct was highly offended and complained during our interviews that you, without warning or notice of any kind whatsoever, appeared at their homes, demanded entry and interrogated them regarding Mayor

1

17 Felony Charges: NOT GUILTY

Oates. This was done without offering to show a badge or properly identifying yourselves. Only upon demand for such identification did you then "flash" your badge. Each of them stated independently that you demanded that they provide you with their "medical diagnosis", and badgered them when they objected to revealing their confidential medical information.

They complained that you were forceful, argumentative, and demanding during the interrogation, as if they were suspects who had committed a crime.

The Complainants stated the following:

Complainant 1: The Complainant was asleep when you arrived. Another person opened the door. When she spoke to you, you did not show a badge, and only after the conversation did you leave a card. You intimidated the client during the conversation by stating that this was a serious interrogation and she must give you answers, making her fearful that she had done something wrong. You asked her about the use of her Medicaid card by D-Pom and whether she was aware that her card was being used to bill Medicaid for services, including psychiatric medical services. She responded that she was aware and that the billing was with her consent. You then demanded, "What is your diagnosis?" She objected to your demand because she did not know who you were and what your authority was, but because you persisted in demanding her diagnosis, she unwillingly disclosed her diagnosis to the best of her knowledge. You also demanded to know whether she was treated by the psychiatrist, asked about the physician's name and at no time did you tell her why you were asking. You demanded that she tell you anything bad she knew about Mayor Oates, asking her to reveal everything she might possibly know about her. At that point the Complainant was so upset that she demanded that you leave her house. This Complainant told you that she is at D-Pom every weekday from 9-5, working diligently on obtaining her GED, loves the help and nurturing she receives through D-Pom. She added that this service is helping her "to better herself".

Complainant 2: This Complainant is the mother of Mayor Oates' client who was present at all times during your invasion of their home and the forced interrogation. You did flash a badge to gain entry and invited yourself to sit in their kitchen. You demanded information about the use of the daughter's Medicaid card and about paperwork regarding the billing. You then demanded to know her daughter's diagnosis, "whether she is bi-polar or schizophrenic or any other diagnosis". You also demanded information on her daughter's physicians, and whether your daughter actually attends D-Pom. They responded that the daughter attends D-Pom daily. The mother felt intimidated into revealing her daughter's diagnosis, leaving her very upset. You then demanded to know anything negative they knew in regard to Mayor Oates.

Complainant 3: This complainant was at home and very scared because you kept banging on her door. She had taken her medication and was very confused, "Zombilized", in her words. She stated that a black woman showed her a badge, and a white man showed her nothing, and that both insisted on entering her home. She stated that she was "afraid of you and worried that

2

something bad was happening". You asked her about Mayor Oates and told her to tell you everything she knew about Mayor Oates. When she told you that she didn't know Mayor Oates, you badgered her that they knew she was "best friends with Mayor Oates and you see her all the time". You expressed anger and dissatisfaction with her explanation that she had only seen Mayor Oates' picture on a sign on the highway, and she added that "Ms. Oates was real pretty". She told you that she didn't go to D-Pom any longer, but when she went there in the past for psychiatric treatment, she did not remember seeing Mayor Oates, but saw other staff members. You demanded to know her diagnosis and asked her "Are you crazy... Are you crazy?" This made her very upset, and she told you that she didn't know her diagnosis because it was too complicated. You left her with the fear that she had committed some crime.

Complainant 4: You came to her house and pounded on the door without stopping. She was alone at home and scared when someone persisted in banging on the door. She was in bed at the time and got up to answer the door. A black woman and a white man demanded entry without identifying themselves, but she would not let them in until they showed their badges. She then unwillingly let you into the house, terrified that she was in trouble for something she didn't know anything about. You had her picture and you told her you had her diagnosis, but nonetheless you kept asking her about her medical diagnosis. She answered because she felt intimidated by you. You asked how often she is at D-Pom and whether she likes it. She responded that she likes it a lot and is getting her GED. You also asked whether she authorized for her Medicaid card to be used to pay for the services, and she answered "Yes". You asked her for negative information about Mayor Oates, everything bad she knows about her.

Notice And Demand To Cease And Desist

This correspondence provides Notice and a Demand to Cease and Desist from ongoing illegal activity within your "power to prevent or aid in preventing" pursuant to Title 42, United States Code, Chapter 21, subchapter 1, section 1986 ("42 U.S.C. § 1986") which provides in pertinent part:

"Every person who, having knowledge that any of the wrongs conspired to be done, and mentioned in section 1985 of this title, are about to be committed, and having power to prevent or aid in preventing the commission of the same, neglects or refuses so to do, if such wrongful act be committed, shall be liable to the party injured, or his legal representatives, for all damages caused by such wrongful act, which such person by reasonable diligence could have prevented."

Attempting to cause a person to do something by telling that person that such action is required by law, when it is not required by law, may be a felony.

18 USC §242 provides that "whoever, under color of any law, statute, ordinance, regulation, or custom, willfully subjects any person in any State, Territory, Commonwealth, Possession, or District to the deprivation of any rights, privileges, or immunities secured or protected by the

3

17 Felony Charges: NOT GUILTY

Constitution or laws of the United States ... shall be fined under this title or imprisoned not more than one year, or both."

18 USC §245 provided that "Whoever, whether or not acting under color of law, intimidates or interferes with any person from participating in or enjoying any benefit, service, privilege, program, facility, or activity provided or administered by the United States; [or] applying for or enjoying employment, or any perquisite thereof, by any agency of the United States; shall be fined under this title, or imprisoned not more than one year, or both."

42 USC §1983 provides that "every person who, under color of any statute, ordinance, regulation, custom, or usage, of any State or Territory or the District of Columbia, subjects, or causes to be subjected, any citizen of the United States or other person within the jurisdiction thereof to the deprivation of any rights, privileges, or immunities secured by the Constitution and laws, shall be liable to the party injured in an action at law, suit in equity, or other proper proceeding for redress."

Your Violations of Citizens' Civil Rights

United States Constitution, Fourth Amendment:
"The right of the people to be secure in their persons, houses, papers, and effects, against unreasonable searches and seizures, shall not be violated, and no warrants shall issue, but upon probable cause, supported by oath or affirmation, and particularly describing the place to be searched, and the persons or things to be seized."

HIPAA VIOLATIONS:
Coerced Disclosures PHI

Federal law provides that people have a right to keep their health information private, including information about their diagnosis. Under HIPAA (Health Insurance Portability and Accountability Act), law enforcement agents are required to obtain written, or a freely provided authorization to obtain a person's diagnosis, when there is no court order, or subpoena or some exigent or emergency circumstances. (See HIPAA Privacy Rules: 42 CFR Part 2§164.501-§164.512(k) et seq.

The Law of Interrogation in North Carolina
The Due Process Clauses of the Fifth and Fourteenth Amendments of the United States Constitution concern state action. Coercive police activity is evidence of involuntariness. *Colorado v. Connelly*, 479 U.S. 157 (1986)

4

Priscilla E. Oates

Were Complainants Suspects?

You, in your role as SBI agents, never informed these complainants of your purpose in interrogating them, nor did you inform them whether they were suspects in some alleged criminal conduct. This failure to disclose your purpose for the unannounced and unrelenting interrogation is part of the circumstances creating the coercion of their Private Health Information ("PHI"), which is protected under HIPAA and federal law.

A suspect's statement is voluntary if it is "'the product of an essentially free and unconstrained choice by its maker.'" *State v. Wilkerson*, 363 N.C. 382 (quoting *Culombe v. Connecticut*, 367 U.S. 568 (1961)). A suspect's statement is involuntary, or coerced, and under the Due Process Clause, when the suspect's "will [is] overborne." *Dickerson v. United States*, 530 U.S. 428 (2000)

When determining whether a statement is voluntary, a civil and criminal courts must consider all relevant totality of circumstances. *Dickerson*, supra; *Withrow v. Williams*, 507 U.S. 680 (1993) Mental or physical. Coercion may be mental or physical. For example, a threat of violence may be coercive even if unaccompanied by actual violence. *Arizona v. Fulminante*, 499 U.S. 279 (1991). Personal characteristics of the suspect may be relevant. Id. Stating that the suspect's low intelligence and lack of education tended to "support a finding of coercion". Id

One of the complainants stated, with facial and bodily expressions of total exasperation, that you asked her: "Are you crazy" Are you crazy"? She related that you kept repeating this question as you pried and repeatedly demanded her diagnosis.

HIPAA permits law enforcement to obtain a person's PHI for the following:
- **To comply with a court order or court-ordered warrant, a subpoena or summons issued by a judicial officer, or a grand jury subpoena.** (45 CFR 164.512(f)(1)(ii)(A)-(B))**To respond to an administrative request**, such as an administrative subpoena or investigative demand or other written request from a law enforcement official but the Privacy Rule requires all administrative requests to include or be accompanied by a written statement that the information requested is relevant and material, specific and limited in scope, and de-identified information cannot be used (45 CFR 164.512(f)(1)(ii)(C)).
- **To respond to a request for PHI for purposes of identifying or locating a suspect, fugitive, material witness or missing person;** may be disclosed in response to a court order, warrant, or written administrative request (45 CFR 164.512(f)(2)).
- **About a suspected perpetrator of a crime when the report is made by the victim who is a member of the covered entity's workforce** (45 CFR 164.502(j)(2));
- **To identify or apprehend an individual who has admitted participation in a violent crime** (45 CFR 164.512(j)(1)(ii)(A), (j)(2)-(3)).

5

17 Felony Charges: NOT GUILTY

- **To respond to a request for PHI about a victim of a crime, and the victim agrees.** (45 CFR 164.512(f)(3)).

None of these legally authorized methods to obtain a persons' PHI are applicable to the manner in which you forced these complainants to disclose their Private Health Information to you. You forced information from innocent and helpless people by intimidation and under the pretense of having a right to do so, preying on their lack of knowledge of their rights. Although you may have thought them unworthy of explanation and easy targets because you think them defective in some way, they are citizens with rights and the understanding that you were doing something wrong to them. The complainants expressed that they were very well aware of your disdain for them and felt hurt and insulted by you.

The SBI shall notify the Office of the Attorney General of North Carolina of each request for inspection of medical records maintained by the Department. *NC General Statutes §90-113.64(c-e).*

Your actions are sadly reflective of a history, pattern, practice, custom and policy of SBI abuses, including the following news reports:

History Of SBI Violations

(1) The recent State Bureau of Investigation (SBI) scandal, where the SBI withheld or distorted evidence in about 200 cases that otherwise could have helped the defendants. See, e.g., Mandy Locke, Joseph Neff, and J. Andrew Curliss, "Scathing SBI audit says 230 cases tainted by shoddy investigations," http://www.newsobserver.com/2010/08/19/635632/scathing-sbi-audit-says-230-cases.html

(2) Settlement means another $1.475 million for Floyd Brown.
Anson County and its insurers reached a $1.475 million settlement with Floyd Brown, the second settlement reached with the mentally disabled man jailed in a psychiatric hospital for 14 years based on an implausible confession. Brown has been compensated a total of $9.325 million from Anson County...

(3) The N.C. State Bureau of Investigation and its insurers have agreed to pay $12.475 million to two innocent men who spent a total of 31 years behind bars.
http://www.newsobserver.com/agents_secrets/#storylink=cpy

(4) Judge order says Michael Peterson's rights violated by SBI agent.
The conviction in 2003 of Durham novelist Michael Peterson was obtained with "materially misleading" and "deliberately false" testimony from a State Bureau of Investigation agent who was a crucial witness about blood evidence in the murder case that spawned TV movies.
http://www.newsobserver.com/agents_secrets/#storylink=cpy

6

Retaliation

Any retaliation against Complainants for exercising their First Amendment Rights of Free Speech by complaining about your conduct, including the complaints stated herein, would also be a violation of their civil rights, actionable under 42 U.S.C. Sections 1983, 1985 and 1986 against you personally, including punitive damages.

Qualified Immunity

The doctrine of qualified immunity protects government officials "from liability for civil damages insofar as their conduct does not violate clearly established statutory or constitutional rights of which a reasonable person would have known." *Pearson v. Callahan*, 555 U.S. 223(2009). *Saucier v. Katz* Because qualified immunity is an affirmative defense, the burden of proof initially lies with the official asserting the defense. *Harlow v. Fitzgerald*, 457 U.S. 800, 812 (1982). In *Saucier v. Katz*, the Supreme Court stated that a court called upon to rule on the issue of qualified immunity must ask the following threshold question: "Taken in the light most favorable to the party asserting the injury, do the facts alleged show the officer's conduct violated a constitutional right?" 533 U.S. 194, 201 (2001). If the Court finds that the facts would show the violation of a constitutional right, the next inquiry is to determine "whether the right was clearly established." A constitutional right is clearly established for purposes of qualified immunity if "[t]he contours of the right [are] sufficiently clear that [at the time the alleged unlawful action is taken] a reasonable official would understand that what he is doing violates that right." *Saucier*, 533 U.S. at 202.

The United States Constitution, Fourth Amendment, Fourteenth Amendment and HIPAA are all clearly established, and a reasonable state official would understand that obtaining a United States citizen's Private Health Information through coercion, intimidation and under the color of law is a serious violation of the complainant's civil rights.

Flashing your badge to compel disclosure of HIPAA protected information is no shield to the Bill of Rights of the United States Constitution.

Conclusion

We hereby demand that you immediately cease to badger and intimidate clients of D-Pom and all other targets of your witch hunt against Mayor Oates, and that you provide any and all exculpatory evidence pertaining to Mayor Oates pertaining to any all investigations you and the SBI have conducted.

The Supreme Court held that withholding exculpatory evidence violates due process "where the evidence is material either to guilt or to punishment"; *Brady v. Maryland*, 373 U.S. 83 (1963

8

75

17 Felony Charges: NOT GUILTY

This is a request for Brady disclosure, consisting of all exculpatory or impeaching information and evidence that is material to the guilt or innocence or to the punishment of a defendant. The U.S. Supreme Court in *Brady v. Maryland*, ruled that suppression by the prosecution of evidence favorable to a defendant who has requested it violates due process. This violation of due process, again, is actionable under 42.U.S,C Section 1983.

Very truly yours,

Charles A. Bonner
Attorney for Mayor
Priscilla-Everette Oates

cc: Eric Holder, United States Attorney General
cc: Roy Cooper, Attorney General of the State of North Carolina
cc: Federal Office of Civil Rights
cc: National Black Caucus
cc: NAACP Legal Defense

9

Below is the actual press release provided by Atty Bonner:

Refer to page 256 to read the original document

Refer to page 256 to read the original document

PRESS RELEASE　　　　　　　　　　**FOR IMMEDIATE RELEASE**
PRESS CONFERENCE TUES. 3/24, 2015 @ 10 AM, EDGECOMBE SUPERIOR COURT

Contact CHARLES A. BONNER	RYAN STUMP & SAMUEL RANDALL
LAW OFFICES OF BONNER & BONNER	LAW OFFICES OF RANDALL & STUMP
charles@bonnerlaw.com	ryan@randallstump.com
475 Gate Five Road, Suite 212, Sausalito, CA 94965	1800 Camden Road, Suite 205 Charlotte, NC 28203
Cell: 415.601.0268; 415.331.3070	Cell:704.286.6942 ; 704.619.0728

MAYOR PRISCILLA OATES INNOCENT OF ALL CHARGES!!

In 2013, the State of North Carolina, the Local Government Commission, and the SBI filed 17 felony charges against then town of Princeville Mayor, Priscilla Everette-Oates, while the LGC and the SBI were fully aware and in possession of all the evidence proving her innocence. The SBI and LGC went to the Town of Princeville and took all documents and receipts proving Mayor Oates' innocence, and willfully and knowingly prosecuted her for 17 felonies for a total amount of $5,200 during a span of three years. Each felony carried a state prison sentence of 4 years, meaning that the government tried to send Mayor Oates to State Prison for more than 60 years for a sum of $5,200. Mayor Oates was at all times innocent of all charges of embezzlement of public funds. LGC and SBI knew she was innocent of the charges. LGC had the receipts showing all funds were used for the benefit of the Town of Princeville. Charles Bonner, Ryan Stump and Samuel Randall are the attorneys representing Mayor Oates. Bonner says they begged LGC to turn over the receipts proving her innocence. LGC refused. The attorneys sent an eight page letter, numerous emails, a Freedom of Information Act request, three subpoenas plus a first court order demanding that LGC, the State Auditor and SBI turn over all documents and receipts taken from the town. LGC refused to comply with all these legal demands, all the while further prosecuting an innocent woman, trying to put her in prison for more than 60 years. It took a scathingly worded Order from Judge W. Osmond Smith III, giving LGC a deadline ultimatum to produce the receipts. Finally LGC reluctantly handed over the receipts showing that Mayor Oates had at all times worked for the betterment of Princeville and never used one penny of Princeville funds for her own enrichment. Bonner says that District Attorneys Tonya Montanye and Robert Evans are to be commended for standing in the bright light of justice and dismissing all 17 felonies upon seeing the evidence wrested from LGC by the final Court Order. "This prosecution was a political assassination of Mayor Oates, orchestrated by her political enemies," Bonner adds. Mayor Oates has always been a committed public servant. In addition to serving twice as Mayor of Princeville, she and her husband, both ordained ministers, have operated a food bank for the hungry for more than 10 years. She is eager to resume community service and will immediately work with other concerned citizens to continue her programs of economic development for the historic Town of Princeville, created by newly freed slaves. The plans include a Bioelectricity Generating Plant which will produce revenue of approximately $250,000 a year to the town. Mayor Oates thanks all of the loyal supporters who stood by her throughout this ordeal.

17 Felony Charges: NOT GUILTY

4.
Judge's Order

*Refer to page 256 to read the original document

Below you will find the order of the Superior Court direct from Judge W. Osmond Smith, III on September 22, 2014. The judge ordered the prosecutor and my defense attorneys to go unannounced to the LGC offices and they were permitted to do an onsite visit.

STATE OF NORTH CAROLINA

COUNTY OF EDGECOMBE

IN THE GENERAL COURT OF JUSTICE
SUPERIOR COURT DIVISION
FILE NO. 13 CRS 02056

STATE OF NORTH CAROLINA)
)
       VS.   )
)
PRISCILLA EVERETTE-OATES)
     Defendant.   )

ORDER

THIS MATTER, coming before the Honorable Judge W. Osmond Smith, III, Superior Court Judge, on September 18, 2014, upon the pre-trial telephone conference between Counsel for State of North Carolina, by and through Tonya O. Montanye, and Counsel for the Defendant, by and through Ryan D. Stump, regarding additional discovery materials discovered during Counsel's visit to the Local Government Commission (LGC) office in Raleigh, North Carolina on September 10 and 11, 2014. The Court makes the following findings of facts and conclusions of law:

FINDINGS OF FACT

1. The Defendant has been charged, by way of indictment, with seventeen (17) counts of Embezzlement by a Public Official.

2. This matter was set for trial on September 8, 2014.

3. Prior to the trial date Counsel for the Defendant requested documents from The LGC by way of a public records request and a Subpoena Duces Tecum.

4. On August 19, 2014 the LGC, by and through the Attorney General of North Carolina, filed a motion to quash.

17 Felony Charges: NOT GUILTY

5. On August 21, 2014, a hearing was held during the Superior Court session for Edgecombe County, before the Honorable Judge J. Carlton Cole, during which the LGC's Motion to Quash was denied.

6. Prior to the trial date, Counsel for the Defendant filed a motion to continue the trial and as a basis for the continuance cited the non-compliance of the LCG to deliver subpoenaed documents to the Defendant, as previously ordered by the Court.

7. On September 8, 2014, a hearing was held during the Superior Court session for Edgecombe County, before the Honorable Judge W. Osmond Smith, III, during which the Defendant's Motion to Continue was granted. In addition to counsel for the Defendant and the State, the LCG was also present on September 8, 2014.

8. Further, during the September 8 hearing, mentioned above, this Honorable Court ordered that the LCG comply with the outstanding subpoena issued by the Defendant and that counsel for the Defendant and State be permitted to inspect the LGC's files during an onsite visit.

9. As a result of the Motion to Continue for the LGC's failure to provide documents, the jury panel was deferred until October 27, 2014.

10. While onsite at the LGC, counsel for the State, Tonya O. Montanye, and Defendant, Ryan D. Stump, discovered documents in the exclusive possession of the LGC that are exculpatory in nature. Specifically, receipts that contained business purposes on the back, that neither the State nor Defendant had previously seen or been provided.

11. Counsel for the parties discovered approximately 35,000-50,000 relevant pages of documents in the exclusive possession of the LGC that are relevant to this pending action.

12. The LCG obtained an estimate for the cost to copy the items that had been requested and ordered by the Court to be turned over. The cost is approximately $10,000.00 and according to the LGC would take approximately 7-10 days to copy.

CONCLUSIONS OF LAW

1. This Court has jurisdiction over the parties to this action and the LCG.

2. The Court has become increasingly frustrated by the actions and/or lack of action on the part of the LCG in its response to the subject subpoena.

3. The LCG has been lawfully ordered by this Court to provide documents to the parties to this action.

WHEREFORE, based on the Courts' findings of facts and conclusions of law and for good cause shown, makes the following ORDER:

1. The Local Government Commission shall have until October 3, 2014 at 5:00 p.m. to provide the requested documents to the parties; such documents shall be provided without further unnecessary delay.

2. The LCG shall provide copies of the requested documents in .PDF format on computer discs.

3. The scanned copies shall be legible and complete to include two sided scans of documents reflecting the same.

4. Neither the State nor the Defendant shall be responsible for the costs related to the production of the requested documents.

5. Failure to comply with this Court's order shall subject the LCG and its employees to further action by this Court.

////

////

IT IS SO ORDERED.

This the 22ᴬᴰ day of September, 2014, *nunc pro tunc* September 18, 2014.

Judge W. Osmond Smith, III
SUPERIOR COURT JUDGE PRESIDING

17 Felony Charges: NOT GUILTY

5.

T. Vance Holloman

While I was serving my first term, an audit took place in 2004-2005 and the independent auditor advised millions of dollars that had been awarded to Princeville to assist with Hurricane Floyd relief efforts was not received. Princeville did not receive most of those funds. Instead, the unused funds were returned to LGC, which is under the NC State Treasurer's Office. T. Vance Holloman decided to come after me to try and destroy me by preventing the truth from coming out from Claire Pinkney's audit.

During my second term in 2010, Holloman was afraid my administration was going to rehire Claire Pinkney who conducted the 2004 audit, however, LGC had Ms. Pinkney's license suspended for three years. Then, LGC began to take the books from the town of Princeville even after my administration brought the town out of the red from the previous administration.

I was re-elected for a second term in January 2010 and Ms. Pinkney worked on our audit during my first term in 2004. Why would Holloman and LGC wait until I was re-elected to recommend Ms. Pinkney's license be suspended? He waited four years to contact the CPA Examination Board to have her license suspended. See the below email where Ms. Pinkney shares with me what happened.

17 Felony Charges: NOT GUILTY

CenturyLink Webmail

ipandrews@centurylink.net

± Font size :

Fwd: Information

Wed, May 22, 2013 05:29 AM

✐ 1 attachment

From : cpinkney <cpinkney@triad.rr.com>
Subject : Information
To : Priscilla Oates <priscillaoates@suddenlink.net>

Sat, Jun 05, 2010 11:05 PM

Mayor Oates,

Look at Page No. 72 of this report. This is why these records were destroyed from the Town Hall after Holloman and Burke learned that I had recommended the Town to have these grants reaudited.

There is much more to come. I will NOT STAND IDLY BY while those liars try to paint me as an incompetent auditor. I knew this information then just and I know it now and while I walked away with them owing me, I WILL NOT WALK AWAY FROM THIS ONE.

The FEMA grant on this reported was never recorded by the Town on the general ledger. Who benefited from the receipts the Housing Authority received (and there is more)?

The Princeville Redevelopment Commission? Who the hell are they and name the citizens in the Town who received any benefit from the properties they purchased? What revenues have the Town received to date from the properties they acquired. By the way, you want to check the registration out on the Secretary of State website. I am convinced they bought Anthony Flannigan's black soul long ago.

This political assignation from the LOG to come after me for my license was a very wrong headed thing to do because some bodies are going to get hurt████████

More to come.

CP

Holloman served as the director of the North Carolina LGC (Local Government Commission) which falls under the Office of the Treasury for the state of NC.

The primary function (and goal) of the LGC is to monitor the fiscal and accounting practices of local governments. The LGC, Local Government Commission, is a department of the state treasury board or Office of the Treasurer and is a federal entity. It was created in 1931 by the NC General Statutes Chapter 159 during the Great Depression to address issues within local government

84

finances. Since its creation, the LGC has worked to provide financial assistance and insight for thousands of units of local government which results in significant benefits to taxpayers and the communities.

During the investigation, Atty Bonner ordered a subpoena for LGC to provide documents and other things, however, LGC did not comply with the subpoena at any time. Holloman filed a motion to quash (reject a legal procedure) Atty Bonner's subpoena to release the records, but Judge Cole denied Holloman's motion and the records still were not released!

In addition, my husband and I felt Holloman's motions were based on whether or not LGC continued to be out of compliance with Atty Bonner's subpoena request for the third time. LGC was out of compliance at least three times. How many times can they be non-compliant with government orders and not be held in contempt?

We know that LGC lied and was involved in a conspiracy to hide the documents taken from my office for the town of Princeville. I have felt strongly from the beginning that LGC tampered with the documents and the proof would soon be revealed! We trusted that the motions presented by Atty Bonner would take us to the next level of dismissal of these fabricated charges.

Holloman also instructed Atty Robin Hammond (LGC's attorney) to photograph ALL of me and my husband's privately owned properties. This action moves the discussion from the town of Princeville matters to private matters pertaining to the Oates' family. (See the following pages.)

17 Felony Charges: NOT GUILTY

1   Q   --in your office?

2   A   Sir, I didn't know they existed, so I certainly

3   don't know where they are.

4   Q   Do you know why they weren't produced pursuant to

5   either the Freedom of Information Request Act or

6   Judge Smith's order?

7   MR. RABINOVITZ: Objection.

8   MS. HILL: Objection.

9   A   Sir, I didn't know they existed, so I wouldn't know

10   that either. No, sir.

11 Q   Okay. Now, did you see any videotapes of Mr. and

12   Ms. Oates' persons or any of their properties as a

13   result of this investigation from Ms. Hammond?

14 A   No, sir.

15 Q   Now, are there any other documents that Ms. Hammond

16   could have provided you pertaining to her

17   investigation of the Oates?

18   MR. RABINOVITZ: Objection.

19 A   I'm not aware of anything related to that matter

20   other than this e-mail.

21 Q   Did you send any other investigators to investigate

22   the Oates other than Ms. Hammond?

23   MR. RABINOVITZ: Objection.

24 A   Well, Ms. Hammond is the only person I spoke to

Priscilla E. Oates

1   about inquiring on the liens. Yes, sir. And

2   that's it. Yes, sir.

3   Q   Well, we--are you sure there was no other

4   investigator retained by you that went out and took

5   photographs of the Oates themselves, their persons

6   as well as their properties, from your office?

7   MR. RABINOVITZ: Objection.

8   MS. HILL: Objection.

9   A   Sir, I've never instructed anyone to take any

10   photographs of them or their property.

11   Q   And you believe that Ms. Hammond just took

12   photographs of the Oates' property on her own

13   accord?

14   MR. RABINOVITZ: Objection.

15   MS. HILL: Objection.

16   A   There was no direction on my part to do so.

17   Q   And you believe that Ms. Hammond, who was working

18   for you at your direction--it was your idea of

19   getting the tax liens, correct?

20   A   Sir, it was my idea that if she were in those areas

21   working doing this work for the town to help

22   release some liens against individual's property--

23   it was my suggestion or my request of her to also

24   see if there were any liens on the property in

17 Felony Charges: NOT GUILTY

1   Edgecombe County.

2 Q   So did you want her to help get these tax liens

3   released from Mr. and Ms. Oates' property?

4 A   Well, those liens were not related to the purpose

5   of the various federal grants. This was--this was

6   a matter of--of not wanting to presume that this

7   newspaper article was in fact accurate but rather

8   if we happened to be in the area also check and see

9   if there appeared to be any validity to this story.

10 Q   What liens were--did you instruct Ms. Hammond to

11   assist citizens with getting--what--who--give me

12   the name of the citizens.

13 A   Oh, I don't have the list of the citizens, sir, but

14   we do recall there was a--there was a backlog of

15   those. Mr. Sharp--not Mr.--the town attorney. I

16   can't recall his name at this point. But he--there

17   was such a backload of those, he had not been able

18   to keep up with them. And citizens had expressed

19   concerns to us about these being so far behind.

20   And we in fact did begin to take some of the

21   efforts. It was as I understand--and again, not a

22   lawyer. So I understand there was simply some

23   legal documents that needed to be filed in order to

24   release the liens on folk's property. I believe

The following pages are a few select portions Holloman's court deposition.

There are (2) volumes of his complete depositions. You may use your phone to scan the below QR codes if you would like to read both of them in their entirety.

Vol.1   Vol.2

17 Felony Charges: NOT GUILTY

1　　　　funds and things of that nature would be assumed--

2　　　　control of that would be assumed by the officials

3　　　　appointed by the Commission. For instance, I believe a

4　　　　member of our staff became--not me, but a member of

5　　　　staff became finance director. So the name on the

6　　　　checking accounts, things like that would have to be

7　　　　changed. That was in--in that letter that the mayor did not

8　　　　choose to accept that day.

9　Q　And that, you're referring to then Mayor Priscilla Everette-

10　　　Oates?

11　A　Yes.

12　Q　Okay. When you say that day, which day are you referring

13　　　to?

14　A　The day the meeting occurred and the Commission voted,

15　　　shortly after the vote.

16　Q　July 31st, 2012? July--rather July 30th, 2012?

17　A　The day of the meeting.

18　Q　I see. Now, the LGC has taken control over the finances of

19　　　municipalities, what, approximately five times?

20　A　I believe it's five or--five or six times, yes, sir. And I think

21　　　there's been at least one since I left. There may have been

22　　　one very late. I think

23

24

Priscilla E. Oates

1   the Town of Spencer Mountain was very late in the time I

2   was there. So probably six. Of course Princeville,

3   unfortunately, has occurred twice. So depending on how

4   you count that, yes, I believe--

5   Q   So of the--

6   A   --six, seven times.

7   Q   Okay. So it's a total of seven times including the fact that

8   Princeville was taken over twice?

9   A   Let's see. There was Princeville, Enfield, East Spencer.

10   Q   In fact why don't you go on and give us the names? You're

11   sort of articulating them out loud to yourself.

12   A   Okay.

13   Q   You--

14   A   Princeville was the first. I believe that was in the '90s--late

15   '90s.

16   Q   Approximately 1997?

17   A   That sounds correct, sir. Then there was involvement with

18   the budget for the Town of Enfield. There were

19   circumstances occurring in East Spencer also that

20   required that to occur. There were a situation with the

21   South Brunswick Water Sewer Authority.

22

23

24

17 Felony Charges: NOT GUILTY

1   Q   I'm sorry. South what?

2   A   South Brunswick Water and Sewer Authority. Then I

3   believe the next--again, when this occurred again was the

4   second time with Princeville. And then the Town of

5   Spencer Mountain, which was a town that essentially has

6   no citizens, has no council. And the Commission essentially

7   just became custodian of the funds they had left over. I

8   believe to my knowledge that is it, at least for the time I

9   was there.

10   Q   Now, when you were there when the LGC took control over

11   Princeville--

12   A   Well, the finances of Princeville.

13   Q   The finances of Princeville.

14   A   Yes.

15   Q   You--you literally went in and seized the--all the

16   documents from the town, is that true?

17

18   MR. RABINOVITZ: Objection to form.

19   A   Seized the documents?

20   Q   The financial documents for the Town of

21   Princeville. You went in on July 31st and took

22   control and removed the documents from the Town of

23   Princeville?

24   A   There were certain documents that were removed but

1   not--not all documents and not documents unrelated to

2   finance.

3   Q   Yes. So is it fair to say you took all the documents related

4   to finance from the Town of Princeville on July 31st, 2012?

5   A   No, sir. I wouldn't say that.

6   Q   Okay.

7   A   No, sir. Some of those documents, yes, I believe some. And

8   over time, some documents were moved to Raleigh--

9   Q   Okay.

10 A   --as the progress went--as it moved along. It was not all

11   one day. Everything didn't occur that way, sir.

12 Q   So it occurred where the documents were removed over

13   several days?

14 A   Well, I would say probably several weeks.

15 Q   Several weeks?

16 A   Yes, sir. It was not a--it was simply--there was-- there

17   were--a number of staff went down. There were a number

18   of areas that needed work: the financial records, the bank

19   reconciliations, the accounts receivable for the

20   water/sewer operations. At first a lot of time was spent

21   there in the town

22

23

24

17 Felony Charges: NOT GUILTY

1   hall trying to get those things done. It just depended on--

2   on--on who was working on what project as to which

3   documents it was necessary to take back to Raleigh.

4   Q   How many staff members did you leave to work in the Town

5   of Princeville following July 31st, 2012?

6   A   Well, initially--let's see. I myself, Ms. Edmundson went down.

7   Then we had a--I believe there were five initially. To my best

8   recollection, there were five folks initially.

9   Q   And who were they?

10   A   Let's see. There was myself. There was Ms.

11   Edmundson. I believe at that point Amy Szalaj went

12   with us. She may have been working from the office

13   though. But I believe she went with us initially at least.

14   Q   Amy?

15   A   Amy Szalaj.

16   Q   Why don't you spell that if you don't mind for the

17   court reporter?

18   A   S-z-a-l-a-j is what I believe--how I believe it is

19   spelled. Ken Weeks went with us and Eric Tony--I

20   believe that was Eric's last name--went with us.

21   Q   Eric Thomas?

22

23

24

1	A	Tony.
2	Q	Tony?
3	A	Tony I believe.
4	Q	Tony.
5	A	I know Eric was the first name. I believe Tony was
6		the last name.
7	Q	And how long did you stay in the town when you went
8		down?
9	A	I was down there the first--probably the first two,
10		three days. And I did not go nearly as frequently
11		as the rest of the staff.
12	Q	How long did Ms. Edmundson stay?
13	A	I believe Ms. Edmundson went down on a daily basis
14		for several weeks initially.
15	Q	And how long did Ms. Amy Szalaj--
16	A	Szalaj. I'm sorry.
17	Q	Szalaj. How long did she stay?
18	A	I believe she also went down for several weeks.
19	Q	And Mr. Ken Weeks did you say?
20	A	Mr. Weeks was working predominantly bank account
21		reconciliation. So I believe he may have only gone
22		down a couple of days initially. And some of the
23		records related to those reconciliations were moved
24		to Raleigh, and--and he worked on them from Raleigh

17 Felony Charges: NOT GUILTY

1   I believe is how that played out.

2   Q   And Mr. Eric Tony, how long did he stay?

3   A   I believe he went down for several--several weeks

4   also.

5   Q   And we know that Ms. Edmundson is a CPA. Is Ms.

6   Amy Szalaj?

7   A   No, sir, she's not.

8   Q   She's not a CPA?

9   A   Ms. Szalaj is not a CPA.

10   Q   Szalaj.

11   And Mr. Ken Weeks, is he--

12   A   He is a CPA, yes, sir. And Mr. Eric Tony is a CPA? Yes, sir.

13   Q   Okay. Now, of course the laws of North Carolina

14   A   authorizes the LGC to take over the finances of the

15   Q   municipality if it feels in its discretion that the

16   finances need to be managed by the LGC, is that

17   true?

18   A   There have to be specific findings made.

19   Q   Is there anywhere in that law that says that the

20   LGC has the authority to remove the documents from

21   the premises of the municipality?

22   A   I don't know if that issue is specifically

23

24

Pace Reporting Service, Inc.

Wilmington (910) 790-5599 • Raleigh (919) 859-0000 • Fayetteville (910) 433-

1   addressed.

2   Q   Yeah. I have read the statute, and I didn't see anything in

3   that regard and I thought perhaps you may know of some

4   law that says you had the legal authority to remove the

5   files from the premises of the municipality other than in

6   the statute that you've cited in your documents. Do you

7   know of such a law?

8

9   MR. RABINOVITZ: Objection to form.

10   A   I am--I am not aware.

11   Q   Okay. Now, it certainly was feasible to manage the

12   finances of Princeville with your staff in the Town of

13   Princeville as they were doing for several weeks, isn't that

14   true?

15   A   Well, the issues we had, one is we had at that point a

16   large amount of our staff were devoted to this one client--

17   I mean one unit of government. So there were at times

18   additional work those folks had to perform during the

19   day. So it became more practical in many ways to work

20   with the records in Raleigh and have some of those

21   people remain in Raleigh. Other--other tasks, yes, could

22   be accomplished directly in the town.

23   Q   Now, when the LGC assumed control over I believe

24

17 Felony Charges: NOT GUILTY

1   you said Enville [sic]--

2   A   Enfield.

3   Q   --Enfield--did LGC remove the documents from the Town of

4   Enfield?

5   A   The Town of Enfield situation was--was very different. The

6   Commission assumed control very briefly to pass an interim

7   budget because the town refused to pass one. Then I went

8   down to the town and I worked with the town in putting

9   together a final budget. And then the Commission took

10   control to have a public hearing and pass that--adopt that

11   budget. So in that case, I think I only spent one afternoon

12   working with the town on that budget, one day. And then I

13   believe I took some copies of some records. It was a limited

14   amount of things needed in that case. But that was a--that

15   was a very different situation. The control existed only for a

16   matter of hours on two occasions. It was a very different

17   situation than--than the situation with Princeville.

18   Q   Well, I understand. But my question is did you remove all of

19   the finance--all the records regarding the finances as you

20   did in Princeville from the Town of Enville?

21

22

23

24

Pace Reporting Service, Inc.
Wilmington (910) 790-5599 • Raleigh (919) 859-0000 • Fayetteville (910) 433-

1   MR. RABINOVITZ: Objection to form.

2   A   We--no, sir.

3   Q   Okay.

4   A   As I stated, we--we were working with the budget. We did

5   not--we went down simply for--I went down simply by

6   myself for one day and worked with the town staff and put

7   the budget together. So it was not--it was not necessary in

8   that situation. Enfield was not a--Enfield was not a matter

9   of their finances were in trouble and they were having

10   financial difficulties. It was a matter of their board refusing

11   to come together and adopt a budget.

12   Q   And how long did the LGC maintain control over Enfield?

13   A   Well, again, I think it was maintained briefly on one

14   occasion to pass an interim budget, and then control was

15   assumed briefly to pass the annual budget on two separate

16   days. And that was the extent of that situation.

17   Q   When LGC took control of East Spencer, did LGC remove all

18   the documents relating to the finances to Raleigh from the

19   Town of East Spencer?

20   A   Some--

21

22

23

24   MR. RABINOVITZ: Objection to form.

17 Felony Charges: NOT GUILTY

The following letter was written by Sharon Edmundson, one of the financial directors with the LGC. She worked closely with Holloman as well. The letter clearly shows my administration brought Princeville out of the red in 2010, therefore, Holloman should not have made the decision to take the books in 2012.

It was later discovered during another audit that in 2002 while serving my first term that millions of dollars that had been awarded to Princeville to assist with Hurricane Floyd relief efforts was never received. Instead, the funds ended up in the hands of the NC Treasury Office under LGC. How could that be???? That is one of the reasons why LGC and Holloman refused to comply to the subpoena from the Atty Bonner's office.

The subpoena information would have shown the financial report trend of how federal grant funds were returned to LGC and reallocated for their own use according to the audit completed in 2004. Atty Bonner requested the balance sheet and other financial statements for the prior 10 years, however, LGC refused to provide the documents.

It was discovered later my administration had 7 prior years of our documents in the attic of the town of Princeville attic. Holloman had one of the maintenance men burn all of those documents behind the Princeville Museum. He was instructed to

Priscilla E. Oates

NORTH CAROLINA
DEPARTMENT OF STATE TREASURER
STATE AND LOCAL GOVERNMENT FINANCE DIVISION
AND THE LOCAL GOVERNMENT COMMISSION

JANET COWELL
TREASURER

T. VANCE HOLLOMAN
DEPUTY TREASURER

December 13, 2010

The Honorable Priscilla Everette-Oates, Mayor
Town of Princeville
PO Box 1527
Tarboro, North Carolina 27886

Dear Mayor Everette-Oates:

The State and Local Government Finance Division in its role as staff to the Local Government Commission has analyzed the audited financial statements of the Town of Princeville for the year ended June 30, 2010. We note that the Town has made progress in a number of areas. The Town's audited financial statements were submitted to our office on a timely basis for the second consecutive year, the Town's General Fund balance available increased, and the financial position of the Water and Sewer Fund has improved. We commend the Town's governing board, staff and citizens for these improvements. However, the Town still has serious financial and operational problems that must be addressed in order to further your efforts to improve the Town's financial condition and operations.

We noted that in the General Fund, the amount of fund balance available for appropriation, as a percentage of expenditures, at June 30, 2010 was 15.85%, which represents a significant improvement from the negative 0.61% at June 30, 2009. However, it is still significantly lower than the average of 65.92% for similar sized units. The governing body and staff must continue to take steps to improve the overall financial condition of the Town's General Fund. Fund balance available for appropriation is an important reserve for local governments to provide cash flow during periods of declining revenues and to be used for emergencies and unforeseen expenditures.

The auditor noted both as a statutory violation and as a material internal control weakness that all contracts have not been pre-audited as required nor have they been approved by the Board. State law [G.S. 159-28] requires that all contracts, agreements, and purchase orders include, on their face, a certificate stating that the instrument has been pre-audited to assure compliance with The Local Government Budget and Fiscal Control Act. Failure to pre-audit a contract renders the contract invalid, and the Town should discontinue payment on any contract that has not been properly pre-audited. Continuing to pay against an invalid contract could obligate those officials that authorize

325 NORTH SALISBURY STREET, RALEIGH, NORTH CAROLINA 27603-1385
Courier #56-20-45 Telephone: (919) 807-2350 Fax: (919) 807-2352
Physical Address: 4505 Fair Meadow Lane, Blue Ridge Plaza, Suite 102, Raleigh, NC 27607
Website: www.nctreasurer.com

807

17 Felony Charges: NOT GUILTY

the payments. According to North Carolina State law [G.S. 159-181], any finance officer, governing board member, or other officer or employee of any local government who willfully fails or refuses to perform any duty imposed on him/her by The Local Government Budget and Fiscal Control Act is guilty of a misdemeanor and, upon conviction, shall be fined and must forfeit his/her office and shall be personally liable in a civil action for all damages suffered by the Town or the holders of any of its obligations. The members of your governing board should be familiar with those Statutes that apply to local governments and should conduct themselves such that these violations do not recur.

For the 2009-2010 fiscal year, the Town collected only 76.91% of the ad valorem taxes that it levied, significantly less than the statewide average of approximately 97%. You also should be concerned that this rate showed little or no improvement from the 73.55% reported in the prior fiscal year's financial statements. The Town should work closely with the County to determine what further steps can be taken to increase collections. One thing the Town may be able to do to facilitate garnishment and attachment proceedings is to forward bank account information of delinquent taxpayers to the County. This information may be available from utility account payments made by these same citizens.

Actual revenues in the Water and Sewer Fund were materially less than estimated revenues. When it becomes apparent that estimated revenues will not be received, the budget should be amended to maintain proper control over the Town's operations. Estimated revenues should only include those that are reasonably expected to be realized [G.S.159-13(b)(7)]. North Carolina has very specific guidelines regarding the preparation and adoption of the budget ordinance, and the Town should take care to ensure that it complies with these regulations.

We noted various weaknesses concerning your Town's internal control system that were communicated in writing to you by the auditor. In addition to the low property tax collection percentages and the failure to preaudit and approve all contracts before they were entered into as discussed earlier, the auditor also noted as a material weakness the lack of documentation for some checks, discrepancies in check numbers between the bank statements and the general ledger and an overall lack of segregation of duties. Each of the items noted by the auditor was identified to assist the Board in improving the Town's overall accounting system. We urge the Board to develop a corrective action plan immediately and begin eliminating these serious internal control weaknesses.

The problem areas addressed in this letter require your continued corrective action. Because of the operational problems that exist, the governing board must develop a corrective action plan that details how the deficiencies in internal control that were identified in the compliance reports will be addressed. This plan should be signed by each member of the governing board and copies submitted to us within 30 days of receipt of this letter. We also request that you include in your response a copy any material

908

102

Priscilla E. Oates

amendments to the 2010-2011 budget ordinance. Also, please continue to provide a copy of your monthly interim financial report that is presented to the Board. If you are planning to issue debt that requires the approval of the Local Government Commission, we must have a complete response to this letter on file prior to the Commission's consideration of your debt application. Our staff is available to help you develop your plans if you require assistance. If you have any questions, please contact me at 919-807-2380.

Sincerely,

Sharon G. Edmundson, CPA
Director, Fiscal Management Section

cc: Victor Morrow, Town Manager
Diana Draughn, Finance Officer
Gwen Knight, Commissioner
Isabella-Purvis Andrews, Commissioner
Ann B. Howell, Commissioner
Calvin Sherrod, Commissioner
Petway, Mills & Pearson, CPA, P.A.
C. D. Watts, Town Attorney

17 Felony Charges: NOT GUILTY

On August 26, 2013, I did an interview with the local news after I was indicted, declaring that I was innocent and the truth would be revealed. You may scan this QR code to watch the video clip:

SCAN HERE

Below are the emails and photos which were entered as exhibits to the court. They show the documents and other things taken without permission from the Princeville offices. (NOTE: the quality of the photos are not clear beyond our control.)

This is the proof that the LGC hid, concealed and conspired to seize approximately 50,000 pages/files from the town of Princeville. All of the receipts and documents they claimed I did not have were included in those files. They repeatedly denied to the prosecutor and the defense attorney they had any Princeville files on their premises.

17 Felony Charges: NOT GUILTY

Ryan Stump

Subject:	clarification on pertinent files
Date:	Thursday, September 11, 2014 at 5:47:18 PM Eastern Daylight Time
From:	Robin Hammond <Robin.Hammond@nctreasurer.com>
To:	Tonya.O.Montanye@nccourts.org <Tonya.O.Montanye@nccourts.org>, ryan@randallstump.com <ryan@randallstump.com>

Attachments: image001.png, image002.jpg, FW: photo 2.eml, FW: photo 1.eml

I am attaching photos of two groups of files for which I need clarification whether you want the contents copied.

Thanks.

(Ms.) Robin M. Hammond, Esq.
Assistant General Counsel
NC Department of State Treasurer
State and Local Government Finance Division
4505 Fair Meadow Lane, Ste. 102
Raleigh, NC 27607
Phone: (919) 807-2368
Fax: (919) 807-2352
Robin.Hammond@nctreasurer.com
www.nctreasurer.com
Find us on Facebook

DEPARTMENT OF STATE TREASURER

Janet Cowell, State Treasurer of North Carolina
325 N. Salisbury St. | Raleigh, NC 27603-1385

Ryan Stump   Friday, October 26, 2018 at 10:09:15 AM Eastern Daylight Time

Subject: FW: photo 1
Date: Thursday, September 11, 2014 at 4:58:46 PM Eastern Daylight Time
From: Sharon Edmundson <Sharon.Edmundson@nctreasurer.com>
To: Robin Hammond <Robin.Hammond@nctreasurer.com>
Attachments: image001.png, image002.jpg, photo.JPG

Sharon G. Edmundson, MPA, CPA
Director, Fiscal Management Section
State and Local Government Finance Division
Phone: (919) 807-2380
Fax: (919) 807-2398
sharon.edmundson@nctreasurer.com
http://www.nctreasurer.com

Find us on Facebook

DEPARTMENT OF STATE TREASURER

Janet Cowell, State Treasurer of North Carolina
325 N. Salisbury St. | Raleigh, NC 27603-1385

From: sharon Edmundson [mailto:sgeunc@nc.rr.com]
Sent: Thursday, September 11, 2014 4:58 PM
To: Sharon Edmundson
Subject: photo 1

Sharon

17 Felony Charges: NOT GUILTY

Subject: FW: photo 2
Date: Thursday, September 11, 2014 at 4:58:53 PM Eastern Daylight Time
From: Sharon Edmundson <Sharon.Edmundson@nctreasurer.com>
To: Robin Hammond <Robin.Hammond@nctreasurer.com>
Attachments: image001.png, image002.jpg, photo.JPG

Sharon G. Edmundson, MPA, CPA
Director, Fiscal Management Section
State and Local Government Finance Division
Phone: (919) 807-2380
Fax: (919) 807-2398
sharon.edmundson@nctreasurer.com
http://www.nctreasurer.com
Find us on Facebook

DEPARTMENT OF STATE TREASURER

Janet Cowell, State Treasurer of North Carolina
325 N. Salisbury St. | Raleigh, NC 27603-1385

E-mail correspondence to and from this address may be subject to the North Carolina Public Records Law. It may be subject to monitoring and disclosed to third parties including law enforcement personnel, by an authorized state official. IMPORTANT: When sending confidential or sensitive information, encryption should be used.

From: sharon Edmundson [mailto:sgeunc@nc.rr.com]
Sent: Thursday, September 11, 2014 4:58 PM
To: Sharon Edmundson
Subject: photo 2

Sharon

Remember, in the previous chapter Judge Smith issued an order giving the prosecution and my legal Dream Team to be allowed on the LGC premises to inspect and basically look for our files. As it states in the actual order:

While onsite at the LGC, counsel for the State, Tonya O. Montanye, and Attorney for the Defendant, Ryan D. Stump, discovered documents in the exclusive possession of the LGC that are exculpatory in nature. Specifically, receipts that contained business purposes on the back, that neither the State nor Defendant had previously seen or been provided.[Emphasis Added]

Counsel for the parties discovered approximately 35,000-50,000 relevant pages of documents in the exclusive possession of the LGC that are relevant to this pending action.

The LGC obtained an estimate for the cost to copy the items that had been requested and ordered by the Court to be turned over. The cost is approximately $10,000.00 and according to the LGC it would take approximately 7-10 days to copy.

The following pages show the actual subpoena given to Holloman and the LGC ordering them to release the documents and they did not comply. The order was given by Judge Cole.

17 Felony Charges: NOT GUILTY

SUBPOENA

TO THE NORTH CAROLINA LOCAL GOVERNMENT COMMISSION ("LGC")

ALL DOCUMENT REQUESTS PERTAINING TO THE TOWN OF PRINCEVILLE

1. All receipts, documents, notes, invoices, writings of any kind whatsoever, taken, removed, electronically transmitted, or transported from the Town of Princeville City Hall pertaining to any and all expenditures by former Mayor Priscilla Everette-Oates.

2. All receipts, documents, notes, invoices, writings of any kind whatsoever, taken, removed, electronically transmitted, or transported from the Town of Princeville City Hall pertaining to any and all expenditures.

3. All receipts, documents, notes, invoices, writings of any kind whatsoever, taken, removed, electronically transmitted, or transported from the Town of Princeville City Hall, regarding, relating or in any way pertaining to the pending criminal prosecution of former Mayor Priscilla Everette-Oates .

4. All receipts, documents, notes, invoices, writings of any kind whatsoever, regarding, relating or in any way pertaining to the pending criminal prosecution of former Mayor Priscilla Everette-Oates.

5. All receipts, documents, notes, invoices, writings of any kind whatsoever, regarding, relating or pertaining to any and all expenditures by former Mayor Priscilla Everette-Oates that YOU determined were legitimate expenditures for the benefit of the Town of Princeville.

6. All receipts, documents, notes, invoices, writings of any kind whatsoever, regarding, relating or pertaining to any and all expenditures by former Mayor Priscilla Everette-Oates that YOU determined were *not* legitimate expenditures for the benefit of the Town of Princeville.

7. All receipts, documents, notes, invoices, writings of any kind whatsoever, regarding, relating or pertaining to any

proof that any and all expenditures by former Mayor Priscilla Everette- Oates that YOU determined were ***not*** legitimate expenditures for the benefit of the Town of Princeville.

8. All documents proving that any and all expenditures by former Mayor Priscilla Everette-Oates which are the subject of the pending criminal prosecution, were ***not*** for the benefit of the Town of Princeville.

9. All documents reflecting any and all witnesses who will or can offer testimony proving that any and all expenditures by former Mayor Priscilla Everette-Oates which are the subject of the pending criminal prosecution, were ***not*** for the benefit of the Town of Princeville.

10. All documents reflecting any and all witnesses who will or can offer testimony proving that any and all expenditures by former Mayor Priscilla Everette-Oates which are the subject of the pending criminal prosecution, ***were*** for the benefit of the Town of Princeville.

11. All Documents showing or reflecting all Budgets for the years 2006, 2007, 2008, 2009, 2010, 2011, 2012, and 2013.

12. All Documents showing or reflecting all Minutes and all electronic minutes for the years 2006, 2007, 2008, 2009, 2010, 2011, 2012, and 2013.

13. All Documents showing or reflecting all Audit Reports for the years 2006, 2007, 2008, 2009, 2010, 2011, 2012, and 2013.

14. All Documents showing or reflecting all Account Payables reports along with the supporting documents for the expenditures for Victor Marrow, Former Town Manager, for the years 2010, 2011, and 2012.

15. All Documents showing or reflecting all Account Payables reports, along with the supporting documents for the expenditures for Diana Draughn,

Former Finance Officer for the years 2006, 2007, 2008, 2009, 2010, 2011, and 2012.

16. All Documents showing or reflecting all PNC Credit Card purchases, along with the supporting documents for the expenditures, for former Mayor Priscilla Everette-Oates for the years 2010, 2011, and 2012.

17. All Documents showing or reflecting all All PNC Credit Card and Bank Statements, along with the supporting documents for the expenditures for Diana Draughn, Former Finance Office, for the years 2010, 2011, and 2012.

18. All Documents showing or reflecting all Quill's Gas Credit Cards, and any and all other Credit Card purchases, for the period of 2010, 2011, and 2012 for Victor Marrow, Former Town Manager, along with the supporting documentation for the expenditures.

19. All Documents showing or reflecting all Quill's Gas Credit Cards, and all other Credit Card purchases, for the period of 2010, 2011, and 2012 for Diana Draughn, Former Finance Officer, along with the supporting documentation for the expenditures.

20. All Documents showing or reflecting all Quill's Gas Credit Cards, and any and all other Credit Card purchases, for the period of 2010, 2011, and 2012 for the Police Department, along with the supporting documentation for the expenditures.

21. All Documents showing or reflecting all Quill's Gas Credit Cards and all other Credit Cards used for the period of 2010, 2011, and 2012 on Princeville Senior Citizens, along with the supporting documents for the expenditures.

22. All Documents showing or reflecting all Credit Card purchases, along with the supporting documentation for the expenditures for Delia Perkins, Tara Lloyd, and Samuel Knight during the periods 2006, 2007, 2008, and 2009.

23. All Documents showing or reflecting all Quill's Gas Credit Cards and all other Credit Card purchases for the period of 2010, 2011, and 2012 on all Credit Cards used during this period by any Staff, Police Officers, Managers, Maintenance workers, and all Elected Officials.
24. All Documents showing or reflecting all copies of Reginald Smith's contract from 2010 through 2012, along with account payables reports with the supporting documents for the expenditures.
25. All Documents showing or reflecting the Town of Princeville's Board of Commissioners authorization for audits of Robert Segal's contract, including all account Payables Reports, along with the contract, any amended contracts, and all minutes reflecting such authorization.
26. All Documents showing or reflecting the Town of Princeville's Board of Commissioners authorization for Petway, Mills, and Pearson, PA., including all account Payables Reports, along with the contract, any amended contracts, and all minutes reflecting such authorization.
27. All Documents showing or reflecting the Town of Princeville's Board of Commissioners authorization for Petway, Mills, and Pearson, PA for the years 2009, 2010, 2011, 2012, 2013, and 2014, , including all account Payables Reports, along with the contract, any amended contracts, and all minutes reflecting such authorization.
28. All Documents showing or reflecting all Audits, including Investigative Audits and reports from the LGC State Auditor Department, and any other Audits performed on the Town of Princeville for the years 2009, 2010, 2011, 2012, 2013, and 2014.
29. All Documents showing or reflecting the Town of Princeville's Board of Commissioners authorization

for contracts with Allen Daniels Accounting Services for December 2011 through April 2014, including all Account Payables reports, along with all Stipend Pay for all the Elected Officials during the periods of 2009, 2010, 2011, 2012, and 2013.

30. All Budgets, Balance Sheets, Income Statements, and Expenditure Reports for the years 1999 – 2013.

31. All Documents showing or reflecting all reports and accountings of All FEMA Funds received at any time whatsoever by the North Carolina State Treasurer Department concerning the Town of Princeville.

32. All Documents showing or reflecting all reports and accountings of All FEMA Funds received at any time whatsoever by the North Carolina State Treasurer Department concerning the Town of Princeville, which Funds were not spent for the Town of Princeville.

33. All Documents showing or reflecting all accounting and expenditures of all FEMA Funds allocated for the Town of Princeville.

34. All Documents showing or reflecting the Total amount of all FEMA Funds allocated for the Town of Princeville.

35. All Documents showing or reflecting the Total amount of all FEMA Funds spent in the Town of Princeville.

36. All Documents showing or reflecting the Total amount of all FEMA Funds spent outside of the Town of Princeville.

37. All Documents showing or reflecting the Total amount of all FEMA Funds the Town of Princeville Town itself received for disaster relief.

38. All Documents showing or reflecting the Total amount of all FEMA Funds individual citizens received in assistance.

39. All Documents showing or reflecting the Total amount of all FEMA Funds received by Gwendolyn Knight, Ann Adam, and Carolyn Sharpe.

40. All Documents showing or reflecting the Total amount of all FEMA Funds received by Ann Howell, Delia Perkins, and Samuel Knight.

41. All Documents, reports, memoranda, writings of any kind whatsoever from any source pertaining to any individual convicted for misuse of the Town of Princeville's FEMA funds.

42. All Documents, Minutes, reports, memoranda, writings of any kind whatsoever from any source, including any and all State Bureau of Investigations reports, showing or reflecting the Town of Princeville Board of Commissioners' Authorization directing Commissioner Ann Howell and Former Mayor Delia Perkins to write and sign Check Number 1908, payable to "M.G. Brown" in the amount of $50,000.00, dated "6/29/00", drawn on the Town of Princeville's Centura Bank Account. **(Exhibit B, attached hereto)**

43. All Documents, reports, memoranda, writings of any kind whatsoever from any source, including any and all State Bureau of Investigations reports, showing, reflecting or identifying the nature and

kind of "Building Supplies & Materials" purchased by Commissioner Ann Howell and Former Mayor Delia Perkins with Check Number 1908, payable to "M.G. Brown" in the amount of $50,000.00, dated "6/29/00", drawn on the Town of Princeville's Centura Bank Account. **(Exhibit B, attached hereto)**

44. All Documents, reports, memoranda, writings of any kind whatsoever from any source, including any and all State Bureau of Investigations reports, showing, reflecting or identifying records, invoices, or manifest documents of list of materials obtained from "M.G. Brown", showing the nature and kind of "Building Supplies & Materials" purchased by Commissioner Ann Howell and Former Mayor Delia Perkins with Check Number 1908, payable to "M.G. Brown" in the amount of $50,000.00, dated "6/29/00", drawn on the Town of Princeville's Centura Bank Account. **(Exhibit B, attached hereto)**

45. All Documents, reports, memoranda, writings of any kind whatsoever from any source, including any and all State Bureau of Investigations reports, showing, reflecting or identifying the location and destination of delivery of the "Building Supplies & Materials" purchased by Commissioner Ann Howell and Former Mayor Delia Perkins with Check Number 1908, payable to "M.G. Brown" in the amount of $50,000.00, dated "6/29/00", drawn on the Town of Princeville's Centura Bank Account. **(Exhibit B, attached hereto)**

46. All Documents, reports, memoranda, writings of any kind whatsoever from any source, including any and all State Bureau of Investigations reports, showing, reflecting or identifying the nature of the construction for which the "Building Supplies & Materials" were used that were purchased by Commissioner Ann Howell and Former Mayor Delia Perkins with Check Number 1908, payable to "M.G. Brown" in the amount of $50,000.00, dated "6/29/00", drawn on the Town of Princeville's Centura Bank Account. **(Exhibit B, attached hereto)**

47. All Documents, reports, memoranda, writings of any kind whatsoever from any source, including any and all State Bureau of Investigations reports, showing, reflecting or identifying whether Town of Princeville Commissioner Gwendolyn Knight was a resident of the Town of Princeville at the time of Hurricane Floyd.

48. All Documents, reports, memoranda, writings of any kind whatsoever from any source, including any and all State Bureau of Investigations reports, showing, reflecting or identifying the qualifications for Town of Princeville Commissioner Gwendolyn Knight to receive FEMA Funds.

49. All Documents, reports, memoranda, writings of any kind whatsoever from any source, including any and all State Bureau of Investigations reports, showing, reflecting or identifying that the Town of Princeville Commissioner Gwendolyn Knight was

not a resident of the Town of Princeville at the time of Hurricane Floyd.

50. All Documents, Minutes, reports, memoranda, writings of any kind whatsoever from any source, including any and all State Bureau of Investigations reports, showing or reflecting the Town of Princeville Board of Commissioners' Authorization directing Former Mayor Delia Perkins to write and sign Check Number 1611, payable to "Gwendolyn Knight, et al" in the amount of $23,463.50, dated "November 30,2001", drawn on the Town of Princeville's Centura Bank Account. **(Exhibit C, attached hereto)**

51. All Documents, Minutes, reports, memoranda, writings of any kind whatsoever from any source, including any and all State Bureau of Investigations reports, showing or reflecting the Town of Princeville Board of Commissioners' Authorization directing Former Mayor Delia Perkins to write and sign Check Number 1645, payable to "Gwendolyn Knight, et al" in the amount of $600.05, dated "December 21,2001", drawn on the Town of Princeville's Centura Bank Account. **(Exhibit C, attached hereto)**

52. All Documents, Minutes, reports, memoranda, writings of any kind whatsoever from any source, including any and all State Bureau of Investigations reports, showing or reflecting the Town of Princeville Board of Commissioners' Authorization directing Former Mayor Delia Perkins to write and sign Check Number 1753, payable to "Gwendolyn

Knight, et al" in the amount of $464.00, dated "March 8,2002", drawn on the Town of Princeville's Centura Bank Account. (**Exhibit C, attached hereto**)

53. All Documents, Minutes, reports, memoranda, writings of any kind whatsoever from any source, including any and all State Bureau of Investigations reports, showing or reflecting the Town of Princeville Board of Commissioners' Authorization directing Former Mayor Delia Perkins to write and sign Check Number 1585, payable to "Gwendolyn Knight, et al" in the amount of $24,063.50, dated "November 9, 2001", drawn on the Town of Princeville's Centura Bank Account. (**Exhibit C, attached hereto**)

54. All Documents, Minutes, reports, memoranda, writings of any kind whatsoever from any source, including any and all State Bureau of Investigations reports, showing or reflecting the Town of Princeville Board of Commissioners' Authorization directing Former Mayor Delia Perkins to write and sign Check Number 1586, payable to "Gwendolyn Knight, et al" in the amount of $15,000.00, dated "November 9, 2001", drawn on the Town of Princeville's Centura Bank Account. (**Exhibit C, attached hereto**)

55. All Documents, Minutes, reports, memoranda, writings of any kind whatsoever from any source, including any and all State Bureau of Investigations reports, showing or reflecting the Town of Princeville Board of Commissioners' Authorization

directing Former Mayor Delia Perkins to write and sign Check Number 1587, payable to "Gwendolyn Knight, et al" in the amount of $490.00, dated "November 9, 2001", drawn on the Town of Princeville's Centura Bank Account. (**Exhibit C, attached hereto**)

56. All Documents showing or reflecting all reviews and correspondences conducted by the N.C. Redevelopment Center Crisis Housing Assistance Fund submitted to Gwendolyn Y. Knight.

57. All corresponding documents, and investigations that is in writings and electronics from LGC, the Town of Princeville, SBI, State Treasurer Department, and any other agencies during the periods 2006, 2007, 2008, 2009, 2010, 2011, 2012, and 2013.

Holloman ordered for all the files that were in the attic of the Princeville Town Hall to be burned because Atty Bonner subpoenaed the files from 2000 to 2013 and as we know, LGC refused to give the documents to us. (NOTE: Files for prior years were kept in the attic for 7 years or more.)

STATE OF NORTH CAROLINA	File No. **13CRS0256**
EDGECOMBE County	In The General Court Of Justice [_] District [_] Superior Court Division X

Additional File Numbers

STATE OF NORTH CAROLINA	
VERSUS	**SUBPOENA**
PRISCILLA EVERETTE-OATES	G.S. 1A-1, Rule 45; G.S. 8-59

Party Requesting Subpoena: [_] State/Plaintiff [X] Defendant

NOTE TO PARTIES NOT REPRESENTED BY COUNSEL: Subpoenas may be produced at your request, but must be signed and issued by the office of the Clerk of Superior Court, or by a magistrate or judge

Name And Address Of Person Subpoenaed / Alternate Address

TO **LOCAL GOVERNMENT COMMISSION, ATTN: VANCE HOLLOWAY**
4505 FAIR MEADOW LANE, SUITE 102,
RALEIGH, NC 276007

Telephone No. **(919) 807-2350** / Telephone No.

YOU ARE COMMANDED TO: *(check all that apply)*
[_] appear and testify, in the above entitled action, before the court at the place, date and time indicated below.
[_] appear and testify, in the above entitled action, at a deposition at the place, date and time indicated below.
[_] produce and permit inspection and copying of the following items, at the place, date and time indicated below
[X] See attached list. *(List here if space sufficient)*

> **PLEASE SEE EXHIBIT A ATTACHED FOR THE LIST OF DOCUMENTS TO BE**
> **PRODUCED PURSUANT TO THIS SUBPOENA.**

Name And Location Of Court/Place Of Deposition/Place To Produce **LAW OFFICES OF BONNER & BONNER** **475 GATE FIVE RD., STE. 212,** **SAUSALITO, CA 94606**	Date To Appear/Produce
	Time To Appear/Produce **5 P.M. E.S.T.** [_] AM [X] PM
Name And Address Of Applicant Or Applicant's Attorney **CHARLES A. BONNER, ESQ.** **475 GATE FIVE RD. STE. 212,** **SAUSALITO, CA 94606**	Date
	Signature
Telephone No. Of Applicant Or Applicant's Attorney **(415) 331-3070**	[_] Deputy CSC [_] Asst. CSC [_] Clerk Of Superior Court [_] Superior Court Judge [_] Magistrate [X] Attorney/DA [_] District Court Judge

RETURN OF SERVICE

I certify this subpoena was received and served on the person subpoenaed as follows:
By [_] personal delivery. [_] registered or certified mail, receipt requested and attached.
[_] telephone communication by Sheriff *(use only for a witness subpoenaed to appear and testify)*
[_] telephone communication by local law enforcement agency *(use only for a witness subpoenaed to appear and testify in a criminal case)*
NOTE TO COURT: If the witness was served by telephone communication from a local law enforcement agency in a criminal case, the court may not issue a show cause order or order for arrest against the witness until the witness has been served personally with the written subpoena
[_] I was unable to serve this subpoena. Reason unable to serve:

Service Fee $ [_] Paid [_] Due	Date Served	Name Of Authorized Server (Type Or Print)	Signature Of Authorized Server	Title

NOTE TO PERSON REQUESTING SUBPOENA: A copy of this subpoena must be delivered, mailed or faxed to the attorney for each party in this case. If a party is not represented by an attorney, the copy must be mailed or delivered to the party. This does not apply in criminal cases

(Please See Reverse Side)

AOC-G-100, Rev. 5/13
© 2013 Administrative Office of the Courts

17 Felony Charges: NOT GUILTY

Below is the Subpoena Proof:

NOTE: Rule 45, North Carolina Rules of Civil Procedure, Subsections (c) and (d).

(c) Protection Of Persons Subject To Subpoena

(1) Avoid undue burden or expense. - A party or an attorney responsible for the issuance and service of a subpoena shall take reasonable steps to avoid imposing an undue burden or expense on a person subject to the subpoena. The court shall enforce this subdivision and impose upon the party or attorney in violation of this requirement an appropriate sanction that may include compensating the person unduly burdened for lost earnings and for reasonable attorney's fees.

(2) For production of public records or hospital medical records. - Where the subpoena commands any custodian of public records or any custodian of hospital medical records, as defined in G.S. 8-44.1, to appear for the sole purpose of producing certain records in the custodian's custody, the custodian subpoenaed may, in lieu of personal appearance, tender to the court in which the action is pending by registered or certified mail or by personal delivery, on or before the time specified in the subpoena, certified copies of the records requested together with a copy of the subpoena and an affidavit by the custodian testifying that the copies are true and correct copies and that the records were made and kept in the regular course of business, or if no such records are in the custodian's custody, an affidavit to that effect. When the copies of records are personally delivered under this subdivision, a receipt shall be obtained from the person receiving the records. Any original or certified copy of records or an affidavit delivered according to the provisions of this subdivision, unless otherwise objectionable, shall be admissible in any action or proceeding without further certification or authentication. Copies of hospital medical records tendered under this subdivision shall not be open to inspection or copied by any person, except to the parties to the case or proceedings and their attorneys in depositions, until ordered published by the judge at the time of the hearing or trial. Nothing contained herein shall be construed to waive the physician-patient privilege or to require any privileged communication under law to be disclosed.

(3) Written objection to subpoena. - Subject to subsection (d) of this rule, a person commanded to appear at a deposition or to produce and permit the inspection and copying of records, books, papers, documents, electronically stored information, or tangible things may, within 10 days after service of the subpoena or before the time specified for compliance if the time is less than 10 days after service, serve upon the party or the attorney designated in the subpoena written objection to the subpoena, setting forth the specific grounds for the objection. The written objection shall comply with the requirements of Rule 11. Each of the following grounds may be sufficient for objecting to a subpoena:

- a. The subpoena fails to allow reasonable time for compliance.
- b. The subpoena requires disclosure of privileged or other protected matter and no exception or waiver applies to the privilege or protection.
- c. The subpoena subjects a person to an undue burden or expense.
- d. The subpoena is otherwise unreasonable or oppressive.
- e. The subpoena is procedurally defective.

(4) Order of court required to override objection. - If objection is made under subdivision (3) of this subsection, the party serving the subpoena shall not be entitled to compel the subpoenaed person's appearance at a deposition or to inspect and copy materials to which an objection has been made except pursuant to an order of the court. If objection is made, the party serving the subpoena may, upon notice to the subpoenaed person, move at any time for an order to compel the subpoenaed person's appearance at the deposition or the production of the materials designated in the subpoena. The motion shall be filed in the court in the county in which the deposition or production of materials is to occur.

(5) Motion to quash or modify subpoena. - A person commanded to appear at a trial, hearing, deposition, or to produce and permit the inspection and copying of records, books, papers, documents, electronically stored information, or other tangible things, within 10 days after service of the subpoena or before the time specified for compliance if the time is less than 10 days after service, may file a motion to quash or modify the subpoena. The court shall quash or modify the subpoena if the subpoenaed person demonstrates the existence of any of the reasons set forth in subdivision (3) of this subsection. The motion shall be filed in the court in the county in which the trial, hearing, deposition, or production of materials is to occur.

(6) Order to compel; expenses to comply with subpoena. - When a court enters an order compelling a deposition or the production of records, books, papers, documents, electronically stored information, or other tangible things, the order shall protect any person who is not a party or an agent of a party from significant expense resulting from complying with the subpoena. The court may order that the person to whom the subpoena is addressed will be reasonably compensated for the cost of producing the records, books, papers, documents, electronically stored information, or tangible things specified in the subpoena.

(7) Trade secrets; confidential information. - When a subpoena requires disclosure of a trade secret or other confidential research, development, or commercial information, a court may, to protect a person subject to or affected by the subpoena, quash or modify the subpoena, or when the party on whose behalf the subpoena is issued shows a substantial need for the testimony or material that cannot otherwise be met without undue hardship, the court may order a person to make an appearance or produce the materials only on specified conditions stated in the order.

(8) Order to quash; expenses. - When a court enters an order quashing or modifying the subpoena, the court may order the party on whose behalf the subpoena is issued to pay all or part of the subpoenaed person's reasonable expenses including attorney's fees.

(d) Duties In Responding To Subpoena

(1) Form of response. - A person responding to a subpoena to produce records, books, documents, electronically stored information, or tangible things shall produce them as they are kept in the usual course of business or shall organize and label them to correspond with the categories in the request.

(2) Form of producing electronically stored information not specified. - If a subpoena does not specify a form for producing electronically stored information, the person responding must produce it in a form or forms in which it ordinarily is maintained or in a reasonably useable form or forms.

(3) Electronically stored information in only one form. - The person responding need not produce the same electronically stored information in more than one form.

(4) Inaccessible electronically stored information. - The person responding need not provide discovery of electronically stored information from sources that the person identifies as not reasonably accessible because of undue burden or cost. On motion to compel discovery or for a protective order, the person responding must show that the information is not reasonably accessible because of undue burden or cost. If that showing is made, the court may nonetheless order discovery from such sources if the requesting party shows good cause, after considering the limitations of Rule 26(b)(1a). The court may specify conditions for discovery, including requiring the party that seeks discovery from a nonparty to bear the costs of locating, preserving, collecting, and producing the electronically stored information involved.

(5) Specificity of objection. - When information subject to a subpoena is withheld on the objection that it is subject to protection as trial preparation materials, or that it is otherwise privileged, the objection shall be made with specificity and shall be supported by a description of the nature of the communications, records, books, papers, documents, electronically stored information, or other tangible things not produced, sufficient for the requesting party to contest the objection.

INFORMATION FOR WITNESS

NOTE: If you have any questions about being subpoenaed as a witness, you should contact the person named on Page One of this Subpoena in the box labeled "Name And Address Of Applicant Or Applicant's Attorney."

DUTIES OF A WITNESS

- Unless otherwise directed by the presiding judge, you must answer all questions asked when you are on the stand giving testimony.
- In answering questions, speak clearly and loudly enough to be heard.
- Your answers to questions must be truthful.
- If you are commanded to produce any items, you must bring them with you to court or to the deposition.
- You must continue to attend court until released by the court. You must continue to attend a deposition until the deposition is completed.

BRIBING OR THREATENING A WITNESS

It is a violation of State law for anyone to attempt to bribe, threaten, harass, or intimidate a witness. If anyone attempts to do any of these things concerning your involvement as a witness in a case, you should promptly report that to the district attorney or the presiding judge.

WITNESS FEE

A witness under subpoena and that appears in court to testify, is entitled to a small daily fee, and to travel expense reimbursement, if it is necessary to travel outside the county in order to testify. (The fee for an "expert witness" will be set by the presiding judge.) After you have been discharged as a witness, if you desire to collect the statutory fee, you should immediately contact the Clerk's office and certify your attendance as a witness so that you will be paid any amount due you.

AOC-G-100, Side Two, Rev. 5/13
© 2013 Administrative Office of the Courts

Priscilla E. Oates

ONE LEGAL LLC

**CONFIRMATION For
Process Serving**

This is not an Invoice

ONE LEGAL CONFIRMATION FOR ORDER NO.: 1773415	DATE: 7/24/2014

Customer: Law Office of Charles Bonner	**Attorney:** CHARLES A BONNER
Customer No.: 0002632	**Attorney e-mail:** cbonner799@aol.com
Address: 475 Gate Five Road	**Contact:** CALVIN A BONNER
Suite 212	**Contact e-mail:** calbon@aol.com
Sausalito, CA 94965	**Contact Phone:** (415) 331-3070
	Contact Fax: (415) 331-2738
	Law Firm File No.: none

CASE INFORMATION:

Case Number: 13CRS0256
County: Edgecombe
Court: Edgecombe County Superior Court - District 7B
Case Short Title: STATE OF NORTH CAROLINA vs. PRISCILLA EVERETTE-OATES

DOCUMENTS RECEIVED:	**No. Docs:** 1	**No. Pgs:** 15

Subpoena

Party to Serve: Local Government Commission	Service Address: 4505 FAIR MEADOW LANE SUITE 102 RALEIGH, NC 27607

Confirmation Report. DO NOT PAY. An Invoice will be sent later.

Notes:	Services:	Summary of Charges:
Service Status: Served	Priority	195.95
Services will be invoiced later.	**DO NOT PAY NOW.** Total:	195.95

Attached is your Affidavit of Service. The original will be mailed. If you have any questions, please contact:
Customer Support | Phone: 1-800-938-8815
Thank you for choosing One Legal for your process serving needs.

17 Felony Charges: NOT GUILTY

ATTORNEY OR PARTY WITHOUT ATTORNEY (Name and Address):		TELEPHONE NO.:	FOR COURT USE ONLY
CHARLES A BONNER, 85413 Law Office of Charles Bonner 475 Gate Five Road Sausalito, CA 94965		(415) 331-3070	
ATTORNEY FOR (Name): Defendant	Ref. No. or File No. none		

Insert name of court, judicial district or branch court, if any:

Edgecombe County Superior Court - District 7B
301 St Andrews St
Tarboro, NC 27886

PLAINTIFF:

STATE OF NORTH CAROLINA

DEFENDANT:

PRISCILLA EVERETTE-OATES

PROOF OF SERVICE	DATE:	TIME:	DEPT/DIV:	CASE NUMBER:
				13CRS0256

1. At the time of service I was a citizen of the United States, over 18 years of age and not a party to this action, and I served copies of: Subpoena

2. Person Served (name): Local Government Commission, by serving Alisa Smith - Assistant to Vance Holloman - Person Authorized to Accept

3. Date and Time of Delivery: 7/22/2014   3:42 PM

4. Address where served: 4505 FAIR MEADOW LANE SUITE 102
RALEIGH, NC 27607

5. I received the above document(s) for service on (date):   7/22/2014

6. Witness Fees: Witness fees and mileage both ways were not demanded or paid.

Fee for service (including Witness Fees if paid) $:195.95

I declare under penalty of perjury under the laws of the United States of America that the foregoing is true and correct.

Pauline Purvis
One Legal - 194-Marin
504 Redwood Blvd #223
Novato, CA 94947
415-491-0606

Signature: _Pauline Purvis_

Pauline Purvis

OL# 1773415

6.

Beth Wood

Beth Wood was the auditor for the state of North Carolina and held this position from 2009-2023. She was the first woman to hold this position and was also on the board of the LGC and worked closely with T. Vance Holloman and his team. Prior to becoming state auditor, Wood worked with the NC State Treasurer's Office where she approved audits for local governments. She was sworn into her position as NC's first female state auditor in Jan 2009.

Wood had it out for me all along under Holloman's instructions. She was also on the board of the LGC. She told her office to investigate me and the town of Princeville, and she sent all types of false documents and information to the SBI, Attorney General, D.A., IRS and to AP (Associated Press). That's how she released the story nationally.

T. Vance Holloman recommended to LGC to take over Princeville's books in 2012 when the town was 9% over budget and in danger of defaulting on a loan. (WRAL News 2013). (Wood was on the LGC Board.) The loan was approved by Holloman in the administration prior to mine which was in the amount of more than $300,000. The due date fell during my administration.

Please see the following news articles and a portion of Wood's deposition that document some of the heinous things she did which demonstrate her character flaws.

17 Felony Charges: NOT GUILTY

The auditor's office reviews the financial operations and regulatory processes of more than 30 state agencies, municipalities, as well as its public universities and community colleges. State law gives the auditor broad powers to examine the records of those places, and gives her the power to summon people to answer questions under oath.

Wood ultimately paid about $7,700 in out-of-pocket funds to cover repairs and towing related to the crash. She previously apologized for her involvement in what she described as "a serious mistake."

Wood's departure from the 2024 race creates an opening for Democrat Luis Toledo, who ran for the position in 2020. Toledo, an assistant state auditor, recently announced he's running for the seat. At least five Republicans have also announced that they would seek the office in 2024.

WRAL News state government reporters Travis Fain and Paul Specht contributed to this report.

State Auditor Beth Wood was charged Tuesday with using a state-owned vehicle for personal errands — the latest chapter in a saga that has upended the long tenure of a government watchdog who has enjoyed bipartisan support.

Wood used an assigned, state-owned vehicle in 2021 and 2022 for private purposes, including traveling back and forth to regularly scheduled hair appointments and dental appointments out of town, according to an indictment handed down Tuesday by a Wake County grand jury. She also traveled to shopping centers and spas "where she was not engaged in business in her official capacity," the indictment said.

Wood's driving habits and state-vehicle use came under scrutiny following the Dec. 8 incident in which Wood crashed a state-issued Toyota sedan into a parked car in downtown Raleigh. Wood was charged in that incident. The state then suspended her vehicle assignment as police investigated the crash.

After the suspension was issued, she used a separate state vehicle for personal trips, according to an affidavit. An agent with the State Bureau of Investigation presented evidence to jurors, including GPS data, which eventually led to an indictment, records show. Wood was charged Tuesday with private use of a publicly owned vehicle, a misdemeanor, following an eight-month investigation. Some of the trips detailed in the indictment happened before the Dec. 8 crash, some after.

In a statement Tuesday, Wood said she reimbursed the state on a monthly basis for use of a state vehicle that was permanently assigned to her. "I purposely overpaid for my commuting miles to make certain it covered any personal use over and above commuting," she said.

Wood is scheduled to appear in court on Dec. 4. An investigation is ongoing, according to Wake County District Attorney Lorrin Freeman.

3.1 @NCCAPITOL

NC Auditor Beth Wood to resign following new charge over use of state-owned vehicles

Beth Wood, the four-term state auditor who was charged this week with using a publicly owned car for personal errands, plans to resign on Dec. 15.

Posted 5:29 p.m. Nov 9 - Updated 1:19 p.m. Nov 11

Play Video
Advertisement

By **Chelsea Donovan** and **Jack Hagel, WRAL News**

Beth Wood, the embattled state auditor who was charged this week with using publicly owned vehicles for personal errands, will resign before the end of her term, she told WRAL News Thursday.

The decision caps a stunning yearlong fall for the Democrat who has earned bipartisan support for her work as a government watchdog, ensuring public resources are used appropriately over four terms.

In a statement supplied by her lawyer, Wood said she would step down on Dec. 15 after 30 years of service to the state. "I made this decision because we have such a great team doing incredibly important work and I don't want to be a distraction," she said in the statement. "It has been an honor and privilege to work with such a talented staff and to serve the citizens of this great state."

Wood was charged Tuesday with a misdemeanor after an eight-month probe by the State Bureau of Investigation found that she used at least one state-owned vehicle for private purposes in 2021 and 2022, including traveling back and forth to regularly scheduled hair appointments and dental appointments.

She also traveled to shopping centers and spas "where she was not engaged in business in her official capacity," according to an indictment handed down Tuesday by a Wake County grand jury. An investigation is ongoing.

State Auditor Beth Wood charged in state vehicle case
Wood's driving habits and state-vehicle use came under scrutiny following the Dec. 8 incident in which Wood crashed a state-issued Toyota sedan into a parked car in downtown Raleigh. Wood was charged in that incident. The state then suspended her vehicle assignment as police investigated the crash. After the suspension was issued, she used a separate state vehicle for personal trips, according to an affidavit.
In a statement Tuesday, Wood said she reimbursed the state on a monthly basis for use of a state vehicle that was permanently

assigned to her. "I purposely overpaid for my commuting miles to make certain it covered any personal use over and above commuting," she said.

Wake County District Attorney Lorrin Freeman said her office still plans to prosecute the case and the charges remain pending. She declined to discuss possible plea negotiations, citing professional conduct rules.

Wood, who is scheduled to appear in court on Dec. 4, announced last week that she wouldn't seek a fifth term as state auditor. She told legislators during a Nov. 1 public oversight hearing, noting at the time that she didn't plan on leaving office until the end of her term in January 2025.

"There are some circumstances that are in my life," Wood told the House Oversight Committee, which was meeting as part of an inquiry into the state unemployment office. "And I recognize four years from now I will be 74 years old. So if there are some things I want to do. I need to get them done now."

It's up to Democratic Gov. Roy Cooper to pick a new auditor to replace Wood, according to the state constitution. Whoever he picks will serve until voters select who they want to take over the office, which is up for election in 2024. Asked about it Thursday, before the news became official, Cooper declined to comment.

"The governor respects her decision and thanked her for her years of service to North Carolina," Cooper spokesman Jordan Monaghan said in a statement later in the day. "Our office will have more information about the appointment process for this position in the coming days."

Wood told WRAL in an interview last week that she wants to start a second career on the public speaking circuit.

Scrutiny on driving

The state auditor's job is to make sure government programs are using their resources as efficiently as possible while complying with state and federal regulations.

In 2019 Wood took the state's Motor Fleet Management Division to task for failing to keep a close enough eye on vehicle usage, reporting in audit that 61 of the state's then 7,688 permanently assigned vehicles were assigned to people no longer employed by the state. Seven were assigned to employees without a valid North Carolina driver's license, the report said.

That audit also criticized the state's Motor Fleet Management division for failing to ensure state agencies complied with commuter requirements. The report laid out several examples of unauthorized commuting and recommended that the state take a tighter rein on the issue. Among other things, the audit complained that the state wasn't conducting periodic inspections of vehicle assignments or going over travel logs to identify misuse.

Departing North Carolina Auditor Beth Wood Pleads Guilty to Misusing State Vehicle, Gets Probation

North Carolina State Auditor Beth Wood has pleaded guilty to two misdemeanors for misusing a state-issued vehicle for personal activities

By Associated Press

Dec. 15, 2023, at 11:39 a.m.

ROBERT WILLETT

FILE - North Carolina State Auditor Beth Wood makes an appearance in Wake County Court, March 23, 2023, in Raleigh, N.C. Wood has pleaded guilty to two misdemeanors accusing her of misusing a state-issued vehicle for personal activities. The plea and resulting 12 months of unsupervised probation happened in Wake County court on Friday, Dec. 15, the day she said last month she would resign from the post she's held for 15 years. (Robert Willett/The News & Observer via AP, File)

RALEIGH, N.C. (AP) — On her last day on the job, North Carolina State Auditor Beth Wood pleaded guilty Friday to two misdemeanors for misusing a state-issued vehicle for personal activities.

Wake County Superior Court Judge Paul Ridgeway sentenced Wood to 12 months of unsupervised probation on the counts, news outlets reported. Wake District Attorney Lorrin Freeman said that Wood had paid $1,064 in restitution as part of a plea agreement.

17 Felony Charges: NOT GUILTY

The sentencing and her resignation appear to complete a year in which Wood's driving ultimately led to her departure as auditor, an office she was first elected to in 2008. Wood announced her resignation last month, two days after a grand jury indicted her on the charges.

Freeman told Ridgeway that in 2021 and 2022, Wood used her state-assigned car for more than a dozen trips to a hair salon in Fayetteville, North Carolina, more than 40 shopping trips to Knightdale, North Carolina, and over two dozen trips to two Raleigh spas.

Wood, a Democrat, said last month that she had reimbursed the state to cover personal use of the car by purposely overpaying for miles in which she commuted to her job. Wood's attorney Roger Smith Jr. said Friday that she accepted responsibility for driving her state car for personal use.

"This is a sad day for Beth Wood," Smith said in a statement. "For the past 15 years, she has been honored to serve the people of this state. She absolutely loved her job and is thankful for the opportunity to have served. She has paid a heavy price, but she looks forward to her next chapter."

While auditor, Wood was apt to receive praise or scorn from officials from both parties for reviews from her agency that criticized the misuse of government funds.

The following pages are part of Beth Wood's deposition.

If you would like to read it in its entirety, you may click on this QR code:

17 Felony Charges: NOT GUILTY

1   Q During your office hours when you're in the Office

2   of the State Auditor, would people come to you and

3   talk to you about the investigation?

4   A No.

5   Q Okay. Would reports come across your desk for your

6   review?

7   A About?

8   Q About the investigation into Princeville by your

9   office.

10 A Not other than status reports on all investigations

11   done by the investigative unit. So I can't say that

12   Princeville was never mentioned from a status

13   perspective, which is done quarterly.

14 Q Okay. And the status reports, what's included in

15   the status report?

16 A The stage of the investigation.

17 Q Okay. Is there any difference in handling an

18   investigation that deals with elected officials

19   versus just employees of a town?

20 A Clarify your question, please.

21 Q Sure. If the investigation--let's say, for

22   example, in the status report it says, "We're now

23   going to go and investigate the mayor of a town

24   versus a town clerk," is there anything different

1   or special about that case, or are all the cases the

2   same?

3   A All the cases are the same.

4   Q Okay. In the investigation by your office, are law

5   enforcement agencies included in the investigation

6   typically?

7   A I'm not sure what you're asking me.

8   Q Okay. Well, your office has the fourteen

9   investigators, and they're highly trained and they

10 have lots of experience. They go and investigate

11 these allegations. Do they involve law enforcement

12 officers with them to do interviews or to hunt down

13 documents or things like that, or is it the

14 auditor's job to do all of that?

15 A They can involve law enforcement agencies.

16 Q And who would make the determination to involve law

17 enforcement to assist your office?

18 A The director of the investigative unit.

19 Q So in the case of the investigation into

20 Princeville, Mr. King?

21 A Yes.

22 Q Is that something that Mr. King would relay to you

23 in some fashion?

24 A Not necessarily.

17 Felony Charges: NOT GUILTY

1   Q   Okay. Specifically with the Town of Princeville,

2   did he relay that the SBI was also involved?

3   A   Yes.

4   Q   Okay. And when did he do that?

5   A   I cannot tell you that. I don't know.

6   Q   What was your understanding of why the SBI became

7   involved with the investigation conducted by Mr.

8   Long?

9   A   I don't know that there was a reason given. I

10   don't remember that there was a reason given. But

11   I was just informed that they were.

12   Q   The investigators that work in your office, when

13   they start an investigation, would you say that

14   they go into the investigation objectively,

15   meaning that if they find evidence one way, they

16   go that way; if they find evidence to the

17   contrary, they go that way?

18   A   That is absolutely the direction of the state

19   auditor's office. It is what we stand for. It's

20   who we are.

21   Q   And that's also the investigative--

22   A   Absolutely.

23   Q   --section of your office? Who determines the scope

24   of the

1   investigation for the investigators specifically

2   with Princeville?

3 A   They're given the information, and the supervisor

4   and director determine the scope.

5 Q   And during an investigation, if other things are

6   uncovered that fall outside of the scope, what are

7   they supposed to do?

8 A   It depends. If it takes them down the trail that's

9   within their--what they're doing, then they would

10   continue on. So, again, they can't ignore it if

11   they uncover something that needs to be looked at.

12   I mean, again, you just don't draw the lines around

13   the scope and say, "This is it."

14 Q   Okay. And the scope of the investigation into

15   Princeville was related to FEMA funds and to the

16   town finances?

17 A   Yes.

18 Q   Okay. Do the auditors in your office do their own

19   investigations, or do they rely on--on other

20   people's investigations?

21 A   Could you clarify that for me, please?

22 Q   Sure. And specifically as to Mr. Long, he was

23   investigating allegations of FEMA funds and their

24   misuse. As part of his investigation, would he

Ms. Wood   Direct   -34-

1   have been required to actually investigate it,

2   or could he rely on a different agency's

3   investigation?

4 A   I apologize. I'm not following.

5   MR. RANDALL: Okay. In your--we'll mark these.

6   We'll mark these as Desposition Exhibit No.

7   1.

8   (DEPOSITION EXHIBIT NO. 1

9   MARKED FOR IDENTIFICATION)

10   MR. LINDSLEY: Thank you.

11 Q   Here you go. And Ms. Wood, Deposition Exhibit

12   No. 1, that is the April 2013 report from your

13   office. Is that correct?

14   MR. LINDSLEY: Go through the document if

15   you need to.

16 A   (Examines paperwritings.) Yes.

17 Q   And as part of the--I guess the introduction, it

18   says, "Through the July 30, 2012 special meeting of

19   the LGC"--and this is where I believe earlier you

20   relayed that you had been provided information

21   about the FEMA money in that. Did you ever talk

22   with Mr. Long about the FEMA money and--and the

23   investigation into that?

24 A   No.

1   MR. LINDSLEY: Counselor, I need to

2   correct one thing.

3   MR. RANDALL: Sure.

4   MR. LINDSLEY: I think you said where she

5   said she received FEMA money. I don't think her

6   testimony was that she received any money.

7 Q And I apologize. The information about FEMA money

8   from Ms. Oates. That happened at the LGC July 30,

9   2012 meeting, correct?

10 A You're saying it's FEMA money. I was handed a copy

11   of a check that referenced some allegations. So

12   would you repeat your question? I apologize.

13 Q Sure. I'll make it a little more general. At the

14   July 30, 2012 LGC meeting, that is where Ms. Oates

15   gave a packet of information to you, including a

16   fifty thousand--a copy of a fifty-thousand-dollar

17   check and some other allegations about misuse of

18   money?

19   MR. LINDSLEY: Objection.

20 A I need to stop you there.

21 Q Sure.

22 A I remember the copy of the fifty-thousand-dollar

23   check.

24 Q Okay.

17 Felony Charges: NOT GUILTY

1   A   I don't remember any other documents.

2   Q   Okay.

3   A   I'm just--I'm just wanting to make sure that no

4   assumptions are being made.

5   Q   Oh, absolutely not.

6   A   So I just remember-- And I don't want you to assume

7   Q   anything.

8   A   I appreciate that. I just remember the fif--the copy

9   of the fifty-thousand-dollar check. And there were

10   conversations--again, the--there was a lot of

11   emotion in the room as a result of the decisions of

12   the Local Government Commission, so there was a lot

13   of fast talking and heightened emotions in the

14   conversation. So I'm remembering the copy of the

15   fifty-thousand-dollar check and some allegations of

16   people--commissioners, somebody--getting--building a

17   room on their house or something to that effect. So

18   I just don't want you to think that everything that

19   I'm saying was documented on a piece of paper that

20   was handed to me, I guess is what I'm trying to

21   clear up.

22   Q   Okay.

23   A   So I'm sorry. I interrupted you. But go ahead.

24   Q   No. That--that's okay. And--and I guess that--

1 2   what do you recall? Did you have conversation with

3 4   Ms. Oates on July the 30th, 2012 at the LGC

5 6   meeting?

7 8 A   Yes. It was initiated, though, by a commissioner,

9   and Ms. Oates stepped into the conversation. Okay.

10 Q   Who was that commissioner? I don't remember her

11   name. Okay. But you remember it was a woman? Yes.

12 A   Okay. And what do you recall about the

13 Q   conversation with Ms. Oates?

14 A   Well, I think it was the commissioner, really, who

15   was talking about another commissioner. I think I

16   remember conversations around the money.

17 Q   And just let me be clear. When you say

18   "commissioner," you mean--

19 A   I'm sorry.

20 Q   --LGC commissioner?

21 A   You're right. No, no, no, no. You're right.

22   Thank you. The town commissioner.

23 Q   Okay. A Princeville--

24 A   Yes.

    Q   --commissioner?

    A   Yes.

17 Felony Charges: NOT GUILTY

1   Q   Okay.

2   A   That somebody had received monies and used it to add

3   a room onto a house, I believe is the way the

4   conversation went. And then there was something

5   about a fifty-thousand-dollar check for building

6   supplies.

7   Q   Okay.

8   A   And then Ms. Oates stepped into the conversation,

9   and I believe she's the one that had the copy of

10   the check.

11 Q   Okay. And the--the item or items that Ms. Oates--

12   or Mrs. Oates presented to you, would you have

13   given that to Mr. King?

14 A   I took them back to the office and gave them to Mr.

15   King.

16 Q   Okay. Would that--would those allegations go

17   through the--I guess the vetting, the triage

18   process that you talked about?

19 A   Yes.

20 Q   Okay. So the interaction that--I guess at that

21   point was like a hotline tip?

22 A   Yes.

23 Q   Okay. So Deposition Exhibit No. 1, I guess for

24   lack of a better way to put it, this is the final

1   product of the investigation once the report comes

2   out? Would that be a fair way to say it? Are you

3 A saying this report or in general? In general. Once

4 Q the report comes out and you sign off on it, that's

5   kind of the--the culmination of all the efforts of

6   your office? I'm thinking.

7 A Okay.

8 Q I apologize. But there is a response that has to--

9 A that is published with the report. So yes, the

10   report is the end, plus the response.

11   Right. But, I mean, you get--

12 Q Okay.

13 A You get the response to the report--

14 Q And then that is the report. Yes.

15 A --before the--

16 Q Okay.

17 A --final thing--

18 Q Yes. Yes.

19 A --comes out, right?

20 Q Okay. Yes. I'm sorry.

21 A That's okay.

22 Q In generating--and we talked about

23   the response and--and all that. In generating

24   the--the substance of the report, how is that done

Ms. Wood   Direct   -40-

1 within your office and specifically as to

2 Princeville? Would Mr. Long type up the report and

3 then have it reviewed or--do you understand my

4 question?

5 A I do. But it's--when--when everything is finished,

6 there may be others involved in the report writing.

7 But Mr. Long is the one, yes, that as a supervisor

8 would sign off on it, and then it's reviewed by the

9 director. And then once the report is re--is

10 reviewed at that point in time, then it goes on to

11 a writing review team for grammar, punctuation,

12 spacing, subtitles, so on and so forth.

13 Q Okay. What, if any, involvement do you have in

14 that process?

15 A I review the draft report before it goes for

16 presentation to whoever was investigated or

17 audited.

18 Q Okay. So just so I understand, so Mr. Long would

19 type up his initial, I guess, draft, then in this

20 case, Mr. King would then review his work. Once he

21 signs off on it, it goes to the--I guess the

22 editors to make sure that the--

23 A The deputy--

24 Q --punctuation and all that type stuff--

7.

Barry Long

This man was the deputy investigator for the state auditor. During the investigation, it was discovered that Agent Lolita Chapman, had not only hidden evidence but also fabricated information during her testimony before the grand jury.

The district court allowed two claims to be filed against Chapman for these reasons and the summary judgment was granted to the defendants (NC Dept of State Treasurer, NC SBI (State Bureau of Investigations, Gregory McLeod, Gwendolyn Knight, Ann Howell, NC LGC, NC State Auditor & Barry Long) based on the fact that Chapman was completely immune from the claims brought about from her testimony to the grand jury.

The following (4) pages are part of Barry Long's deposition where he confirmed Beth Wood was the one who called the 800# which was the complaint hotline. (These are pages 14-17 in the complete deposition.) That is what started the fraud investigation on my business, and their goal was to destroy it. It was unbelievable that it wasn't a citizen, parent of a citizen, a client or anyone else who called the complaint hotline. It was the elected head auditor who alerted the officials and I was in total shock!

17 Felony Charges: NOT GUILTY

1   Q   Okay. So who--were you the complainant?

2   A   No. No.

3   Q   What were the circumstances that you created this hotline

4   complaint?

5   A   We received--anytime we open a new case at our office,

6   we have to fill out a hotline complaint form which contains

7   information such as the source of the complaint, the

8   nature of the allegation. If the complainant provides

9   contact information, we will add that. Those are the--and

10   the date that it was received.

11   And--and this document is called a hotline complaint?

12   Q   Hotline complaint form. Form. And you filled in the

13   relevant nformation into the hotline complaint form?

14   A   i I did.

15   Q   You typed it in?

16   A   On the computer.

17   Q   Okay.

18   A   And--and who was the source? You indicated

19   Q   one item on the form was the source. Who was the

20   source of this complaint?

21   A   The source was listed I believe as one or more

22

23

24

1		members of the LGC, which is the Local Government
2		Commission.
3	Q	And when you say one or more, do you remember the
4		names of either the one or the more? The one would have
5	A	been Beth Wood. And I do not know who the others were.
6	Q	Do you have a best recollection of the names of any other
7		sources?
8	A	I don't.
9	Q	Now, Beth Wood is your boss?
10	A	Well, yes, indirectly.
11	Q	And is she also sometimes directly your boss? I don't
12	A	understand that question.
13	Q	Well, tell us what you mean by indirectly she's
14		your boss.
15	A	Well, there's a reporting relationship. I report
16		to the director of the investigation section, and
17		then that person reports to a deputy. And then the
18		deputy reports to Beth Wood.
19	Q	And who is the director to whom you report?
20	A	At that point in time, it was David King.
21	Q	And who was the deputy?
22	A	I believe it was Wesley, W-e-s-l-e-y, Ray, R-a-y,
23		at that point in time.
24		

17 Felony Charges: NOT GUILTY

1   Q   And so you report to Mr. Deputy Ray, or you report directly

2   to David King?

3   A   To David King.

4   Q   Okay. And does Ms. Wood give you instructions with

5   respect to your duties on any occasions?

6   A   Very seldom.

7   Q   But she does on some occasions?

8   A   Actually, no.

9   Q   Okay.

10 A   My direction comes from David King when he was there.

11   And there have been occasions, not many--I can count

12   them on one hand--over the years when if David is out,

13   then--and she needs an answer to a question--then she

14   will bypass, you know, the--the deputy and David and just

15   ask me to come down and fill her in on whatever her

16   question is.

17 Q   Well, she is the state auditor, isn't she?

18 A   Yes, she is.

19 Q   So ultimately she is the ultimate boss, right?

20 A   Ultimately, yes.

21 Q   She's your second line of report, is that true?

22 A   There is two people in between--

23 Q   Yeah.

24 A   --Beth Wood and myself.

Priscilla E. Oates

| Long, Vol. I | Direct | -17- |

1 Q   Okay. So Beth Wood was the source on this hotline

2   complaint. And what was the--you said the second aspect

3   was the nature of the allegation. What was the nature of

4   the allegation?

5 A   I'd have to look at the hotline form again.

6 Q   What is your best recollection?

7 A   That there were issues with--potentially with the

8   documents that we received from Priscilla Everette- Oates,

9   and there were also issues pertaining to the finances of

10   the Town of Princeville. That's my best recollection.

11 Q   And when you say there were issues with documents that

12   you received from Priscilla Everette-Oates, these were

13   documents that had been seized from the Town of

14   Princeville by the LGC?

15 A   No. That's not accurate.

16 Q   Where--where were these documents when you say they

17   were received? Were these documents that Ms. Oates had

18   provided to Ms. Woods?

19 A   That's my understanding.

20 Q   And where did you get that understanding from?

21 A   From David King.

22 Q   Okay. And that was--you had a meeting with Mr. King

23   about that?

24

17 Felony Charges: NOT GUILTY

The following pages are part of Barry Long's deposition.

If you would like to read it in its entirety, you may click on this QR code:

1   Exhibit 4.

2 A   Thank you.

3 Q   I'm sorry. Here is Exhibit 4 here.

4   MR. BONNER: That one's for you. Yeah.

5

6   Thank you.

7 Q   So now, sir, I'm showing you a document marked

8   Exhibit 4 dated September 19th, 2012. You see this

9   document is from Ms. Sharon Edmundson, the director,

10   fiscal management--

11 A   Yes.

12 Q   --and financial office of the Town of Princeville?

13   Do you see that?

14 A   Yes. You know Ms. Sharon Edmundson? You do know her?

15 Q   I do.

16 A   Okay. And you know that she works for the LGC? I do.

17 Q   And as I indicated to you, the LGC seized the town's

18 A   records on July 31st, 2012. Did you--

19 Q   MR. RABINOVITZ: Objection to form.

20   Did you have any discussion with Ms. Edmundson

21 Q   between July 31st, 2012, the date of the seizure of

22   the records, and the date of this letter, September

23   19th, 2012, regarding the finances of the Town of

24

17 Felony Charges: NOT GUILTY

1 2   Princeville?

3 4   A   I did meet with Sharon Edmundson at some point, but

5 6   I could not tell you it was between those two dates.

7 8   Q   Okay. Tell me about the meeting you had with Sharon

9   Edmundson. Tell me each of the meetings you had

10   with--starting with the first one. What is your best

11   recollection of the first date that you had--that

12   you met with Ms. Edmundson?

13   A   Again, I do not recall these dates that well. I will

14   tell you that I have--we met with Sharon Edmundson

15   and possibly Vance Holloman together on some date.

16   That would be in the work papers documented by a

17   what we call memorandum of interview so that

18   whatever was discussed during that meeting would be

19   in that memorandum, which would be a lot more

20   accurate than me trying to, you know, guess right

21   now about what was in there, what was talked about.

22   Q   Okay.

23   A   I assume you have those documents.

24   Q   I appreciate your assumption, sir, but we may not

    have those documents. Do you--did you review those

    documents?

1   MR. LINDSLEY: Counsel, those--that--that

2   document--

3   MR. BONNER: If you have an objection,

4   counsel, make your objection. I don't--I don't

5   need your speech, please. Just make your

6   objection.

7   MR. LINDSLEY: Well, I don't--I don't

8   need you stating for the record that you don't have

9   documents that have been produced to you, sir.

10   MR. BONNER: If you have an objection,

11   please make it.

12   MR. LINDSLEY: I object to your--

13   MR. BONNER: Okay.

14   MR. LINDSLEY: --implying that you have

15   not been given documents that have been produced,

16   sir.

17   Q   Now, sir, Mr. Long, in preparing for your testimony

18   today, did you review any of these memo of

19   interviews?

20   A   I did one.

21   Q   Okay. And what was the date of the one that you

22   reviewed?

23   A   I don't recall.

24   Q   Okay. And the one that you reviewed today, did it

Pace Reporting Service, Inc.
Wilmington (910) 790-5599   Raleigh (919) 859-0000   Fayetteville (910) 433-

17 Felony Charges: NOT GUILTY

1   reflect that you had a conversation with Ms.--Mr.

2   Vance Holloman and Ms. Sharon Edmundson?

3   A   Yes.

4   Q   Okay.

5   MR. BONNER: And, counsel--Jeremy, if you

6

7   would also produce that document to us, we'd

8   appreciate that. We're entitled to it under the

9   law--under the rules in light of the fact that he--

10   he reviewed it.

11   Q   And, now, what is your best recollection as to the

12   content of that memorandum of interview in that

13   meeting that you had with Ms. Edmundson and Mr.

14   Holloman?

15   A   Sure. My best recollection was that David King,

16   myself and Bryan Matthews, who was one of my staff

17   guys, were at the meeting on behalf of the state

18   auditor's office and that Sharon Edmundson, Vance

19   Holloman and perhaps Robin Hammond were also at that

20   meeting.

21   Q   Okay. And is it your best recollection that meeting

22   was in October of 2012?

23   A   I don't know.

24   Q   Fair enough. You can't remember the date.
             Okay. So at that meeting, you've

Long, Vol. I   Direct   -55-

1   indicated Sharon was there, Mr. Holloman was there,

2   Robin Hammond was there. Was Beth Wood there?

3   MR. RABINOVITZ: Objection to form.

4   A   No.

5   MR. RABINOVITZ: I believe that

6   mischaracterizes what he said about who was in

7   attendance.

8   Q   Obviously you were there, Mr. David King was there,

9   and Mr. Bryan Matthew was there.

10   A   That is correct.

11   Q   Okay. Other than those people that we've named,

12   can you have any recollection of anyone else being

13   there?

14   A   Not other than the people we named.

15   Q   Okay. And those names are reflected in the

16   memorandum of interview?

17   A   They would be, yes.

18   Q   Okay. And who called that meeting?

19   A   It may have been--could have been me.

20   Q   Okay. And why did you call the meeting?

21   A   Well, to try and--depending on when this was--and

22   I'm thinking this was during what I'll call the

23   preliminary phase--just to try and get all the

24   information together as to--you know, more

17 Felony Charges: NOT GUILTY

1   specifics as to what the issues were that might

2   need to be looked at.

3   Q   Now, was this meeting regarding Ms. Everette-Oates?

4   A No.

5   Q   Okay. What was this meeting regarding?

6   A   This had to do with the--the finances of the town.

7   And I don't know if the--if the fifty-thousand-

8   dollar check and the Gwendolyn Knight things came

9   up in that or not. I don't recall that. But they

10   may have.

11   Q   And what do you recall that you said in that

12   meeting?

13   A   Again, I--a contemporaneous account of it is

14   contained in the memorandum, and I really don't

15   want to speculate on that because I just don't

16   know.

17   Q   Okay. Do you have a recollection of what Mr. Van

18   Holloman said in the meeting?

19   A   I do not.

20   Q   Ms. Sharon Edmundson, do you have a recollection

21   what she said in the meeting?

22   A No.

23   Q   Do you have a recollection of what Ms. Robin

24   Hammond said in the meeting?

1   A   No, I do not.

2   Q   And you understand Ms. Robin Hammond is the attorney

3   for the LGC?

4   A   I do.

5   Q   Okay. And do you have a recollection what Mr. David

6   King said in the meeting?

7   A   I do not. And what about Mr. Bryan Matthews? Do you

8   Q   have a recollection what he said in the meeting?

9   I do not.

10 A   Okay. But what each individual said is memorialized

11 Q   in this memorandum of interview, is that true?

12 A   Partially.

13 Q   Okay. Okay. And as a part of your training for your

14   CFE, certified fraud investigator, it is part of the

15   protocol to have a very thorough recordkeeping. Is

16   that a fair statement?

17 A   I don't know that that is part of the protocol. We

18   try and keep good records regardless.

19 Q   It's good practice to have an accurate recordkeeping,

20   particularly if someone's freedom is on the line

21   where you could put--could be referred to the

22   district attorney for prosecution, isn't

23

24

17 Felony Charges: NOT GUILTY

1   that--isn't that true?

2   MR. LINDSLEY: Objection to form.

3 A We do keep good records.

4 Q Okay.

5 A Yes.

6 Q And you did so in this case?

7 A In this entire case.

8 Q Yes.

9 A Yes.

10 Q Okay. Now, in Exhibit 4, if you look through the

11   pages, you'll notice there are some ledgers attached

12   to--it's--(unintelligible)--Page 894 through nine zero

13   three--actually nine oh two. you see those ledgers

14   that are attached?

15 A I do.

16 Q And--and I want to direct your attention to Page 899.

17   Do you see that?

18 A I do.

19 Q And up in the top category, under receipts, yes and

20   no--do you see that up at the top of the page? It says

21   receipts--

22 A Yes--

23 Q --yes and no.

24 A --I see that.

Q   And as a CPA, you're used to seeing these kind of
    spreadsheets--Excel spreadsheets of documents. Is
    that a fair statement?

A   I see a lot of spreadsheets.

Q   Yes. And you see down in the middle of the pages
    there are several yes's indicating that they had
    receipts. See that?

A   Yes. And--and down at the bottom that there are

Q   yes's indicating there were receipts. Do you see
    that?

A   At the bottom of the page?

Q   Yes. Page 899.

        MR. LINDSLEY: Where--where are you
    referring to specifically, counsel?

Q   Down the dates of 5-16-2011, Shell Oil, and it
    indicates all the way down to 5-6-2011 that there
    was yes, yes, yes indicating that they were
    receipts. See that?

A   I'm--don't know if I'm--

Q   Are you on Page 898?

        MR. LINDSLEY: I don't see those dates.

A   I'm on eight ninety-nine.

Q   Okay. Go to Page 898. I'm sorry. Eight ninety-
    eight.

Long, Vol. I   Direct   -60-

1 2 A   That's all right.   So--

3 4 Q   And you see starting at the date of 6-21-2011,

5 6   Shell Oil, there's yes all the way down to the date

7 8   of 5-24-2011, Exxon Mobil, yes, indicating that

9   there were receipts. See that?

10 A   Yes.

11   MR. LINDSLEY: Objection to form.

12 Q   Okay. Now, going down to the date of 5-16-2011

13   down to the date of 5-6-2011, there's yes

14   indicating receipts. Do you see that?

15   MR. LINDSLEY: Objection to form.

16 A   Yes, I do.

17 Q   Okay. Now, and over in the category to the right of

18   that expense report, yes, no, again, there's a

19   number of yes's from the date of 6-21-2011 down to

20   5-24-2011. Do you see that?

21 A   I do.

22 Q   Okay. And to the right of that 6-21-2011, it

23   indicates economic development committee. Do you see

24   all those all the way down to the bottom of the

       page? It's economic development committee--

          MR. LINDSLEY: Objection.

          MR. RABINOVITZ: Objection to form.

  Q   --management meetings?

8.

SBI/Agent Lolita Chapman

This was the financial crimes government agent appointed to handle my investigation from the request of Beth Wood. Her staff's email specifically stated to the SBI (State Bureau of Investigations) that they assign an "African American agent" so the investigation would not appear racially-based. See the below email with this request from Barry Long, the deputy

---

McNeill, Cheryl

From:	Barry Long [Barry_Long@ncauditor.net]
Sent:	Monday, October 29, 2012 4:10 PM
To:	McNeill, Cheryl
Cc:	David A. King
Subject:	Request for Assistance

Dear Ms. McNeill,

We are conducting an investigation regarding fraud, waste, or abuse of public funds in the town of Princeville. It would be extremely helpful if you would be willing to assign one of your Financial Crimes agents to work with us during various phases of our engagement, but especially so during the interview process. We are sensitive to the fact that some people may attempt to portray any investigation of the town's finances as a racial issue. Because of this, the assignment of an African American agent would be preferable in terms of relieving any anxiety on the part of Princeville's citizenry in this regard.

Thank you in advance for your consideration, and we look forward to your reply.

Barry G. Long, CPA, CFF, CFE
Supervisor, Special Investigations
North Carolina Office of the State Auditor
2 S. Salisbury Street
20601 Mail Service Center
Raleigh, NC 27699-0601

Phone: (919) 807-7745
Fax: (919) 807-7685
barry_long@ncauditor.net

WARNING: E-mail correspondence to and from The Office of the State Auditor may be subject to the North Carolina Public Records Law and may be disclosed to third parties.

investigator for the state auditor's, to Cheryl McNeill with the NC State Bureau of Investigations (SBI):

Cheryl McNeill responded to Long's request with the name of the agent who would be assigned:

NORTH CAROLINA
STATE BUREAU OF INVESTIGATION
DEPARTMENT OF JUSTICE

3320 GARNER ROAD
PO BOX 29500
RALEIGH, NC 27626-0500
(919) 662-4500
FAX: (919) 662-4523

ROY COOPER
ATTORNEY GENERAL

GREGORY S. McLEOD
DIRECTOR

October 30, 2012

Barry G. Long, CPA, CFF, CFE
Supervisor, Special Investigations
North Carolina Office of the State Auditor
2 S. Salisbury Street
20601 Mail Service Center
Raleigh, NC 27699-0601

RE: Fraud of Public Funds in the Town of Princeville

Supervisor Barry Long:

In response to your request for an investigation in the above referenced matter, Agent Lolita Chapman has been assigned to this investigation. Agent Chapman will contact you with her findings.

If you have any questions please feel free to call Agent Chapman or myself at 252-756-4755.

Sincerely,

Cheryl H. McNeill
Supervisor in Charge

CHM:jsc

cc: Agent Lolita Chapman
    File

2913-00827
1951-28.1

A Nationally Accredited State Agency

DA000015   An ASCLD/LAB Accredited Laboratory Since 1988

Sharon Edmundson, who worked at the LGC office, provided Agent Chapman with a spreadsheet which advised that purchases had been made with no receipts, if the Economic Development Committee was a legitimate committee. Agent Chapman focused her investigation on that spreadsheet.

Lolita Brown-Chapman, CFE

Special Agent at North Carolina Department of Justice

Raleigh-Durham, North Carolina Area   Law Enforcement

Current	Lenoir Community College, North Carolina Department of Justice, Medicaid Criminal Investigations
Previous	North Carolina Department Justice, Northeastern District Kinston Department of Public Safety
Education	North Carolina Justice Academy

Special Agent
North Carolina Department of Justice, Medicaid Criminal Investigations
January 2014 – Present (1 year 3 months) | raleigh-durham area, north carolina

Special Agent
North Carolina Department Justice, Northeastern District
January 2008 – January 2014 (6 years 1 month) | greenville area, north carolina

She was placed in the Medicaid investigation department to destroy and shut down my businesses based on the false allegations. My businesses were suspended from receiving payments for over a year. Agent Chapman literally harassed my clients to get information to add to all the false claims against me. This was all part of the conspiracy and fabrication originated from SBI, OSA and LGC.

Here is the letter stating the Medicaid payments were

suspended, which meant my businesses would be shut down due to no income.

North Carolina Department of Health and Human Services
Division of Medical Assistance

Pat McCrory
Governor

Aldona Z. Wos, M.D.
Ambassador (Ret.)
Secretary DHHS

Robin Gary Cummings, M.D.
Deputy Secretary for Health Services
Director, Division of Medical Assistance

August 4, 2014

CERTIFIED MAIL
7010 1060-0802 0666 7569

Tarboro, NC 27886-1634

PI Case #: 2013-1082

Subject: Suspension of Medicaid Payments

Dear Provider:

Pursuant to 42 CFR § 455.23(a), the Division of Medical Assistance (DMA) **must** suspend all Medicaid payments to a provider after the agency determines there is a credible allegation of fraud for which an investigation is pending under the NC Medicaid program. DMA has received a credible allegation of fraud against ▬▬▬▬▬▬

The general allegations as to the nature of the suspension action include but may not be limited to:

- A complaint alleging that the provider billed for services not rendered.

DMA is not required to disclose any specific information concerning an ongoing investigation. The State Medicaid agency has carefully reviewed all allegations, facts and available evidence carefully prior to taking this action, and has determined that the allegation(s) listed above have indicia of reliability.

Payments to your agency have been suspended for all claims received by the fiscal agent on or after 8/12/14 in accordance with 42 CFR § 455.23. This suspension applies to Behavioral Health Services Medicaid claims submitted by the provider number(s) listed below. Any attempt to circumvent this payment suspension action by submitting claims for services performed under this number through other agencies, site locations, or billing numbers shall result in termination of your NC Medicaid Provider Participation Agreement.

www.ncdhhs.gov
Tel 919-855-4100 • Fax 919-733-6608
Location: 1985 Umstead Drive • Kirby Building • Raleigh, NC 27603
Mailing Address: 2501 Mail Service Center • Raleigh, NC 27699-2501
An Equal Opportunity / Affirmative Action Employer

Case 5:16-cv-00623-FL   Document 112   Filed 12/20/16   Page 100 of 140

164

Priscilla E. Oates

Provider Name:	
Provider Servicing Address:	████████ Ste 109, Tarboro, NC 27886-1920
	████████ Ste 201, Tarboro, NC 27886-1920
	████████ Ste 209, Tarboro, NC 27886-1920
	████████ Tarboro, NC 27886-1920
	████████ Princeville, NC 27886-9542
Locator Code:	003, 004, 005, 006, 007
PI Case Number:	2013-1082
Legacy Provider Number:	8303306, 8301751
NPI:	1336291699
Taxonomy:	251S00000X Community/Behavioral Health

This payment suspension is for a temporary period. Pursuant to 42 CFR § 455.23(c), payment suspension will not continue after either of the following:

1. The agency or the prosecuting authorities determine that there is insufficient evidence of fraud by the provider; or
2. Legal proceedings related to the provider's alleged fraud are completed.

You have the right to submit written evidence to the DMA for reconsideration. To request a reconsideration review of this decision, please return the enclosed form within 15 business days of receipt of this letter to:

Chief Hearing Officer
DHHS Hearing Office
2501 Mail Service Center
Raleigh, North Carolina, 27699-2501
Attention PI Case #: 2013-1082

You may request a telephone or personal hearing. You may also submit written documentation for review. The documentation must be received within 15 business days from receipt of this letter in order to be considered. If you request a personal hearing, the hearing will be scheduled in the DHHS Raleigh office. Following reconsideration review, you will be notified in writing of the decision.

If you do not request a Reconsideration Review or if you disagree with the reconsideration review decision, you may file a petition for a contested case hearing with the Office of Administrative Hearings (OAH) in accordance with G.S. § 150B-23(a). You have 60 calendar days from the date of this letter or the date of the reconsideration review decision to **file** a contested case petition with the OAH. Petition forms are available on the OAH website at http://www.oah.state.nc.us/forms.html. There may be a fee associated with filing a petition at OAH. If you have questions about the OAH appeal process or the filing fee, OAH can be reached directly at (919) 431-3000. You **must** file the contested case petition form with the Office of Administrative Hearings, either in person at 1711 New Hope Church Road, Raleigh, NC 27609, by mail at 6714 Mail Service Center, Raleigh, NC 27699-6714 or via facsimile or

17 Felony Charges: NOT GUILTY

electronic transmission in accordance with 26 NCAC 03.0101(c) **and** mail a copy to Legal Counsel, NC Department of Health and Human Services, 101 Blair Drive, Raleigh, NC, 27603.

If you have any questions regarding this notice, please contact me directly at 919-814-0000.

Sincerely,

Patrick Piggott, Section Chief
Behavioral Health Review Section
Program Integrity

/maw

Enclosure

Cc: Jeff Horton, Assistant Director of Compliance
      Pat Delbridge, Program Integrity Business Operations
      Richard Brennan, DMA Chief Financial Officer
      Sheila Platts, DMA Provider and Recipient Services
      Sandra Terrell, DMA Chief Operations Officer
      Laketha Miller, DHHS Controller
      Belinda Smith, NCDOJ Health and Public Assistance
      LMEs / LME-MCOs

Below is the actual Indictment/Order Arrest. There are 17 charges listed and each of the charges held a 4½ year sentence in state prison. This is how I was facing 75 years in prison.

For example, charge #17 was for $74.21. (see pg.171) Atty Bonner told me all charges would have to be dropped in order for me to not go to prison. Even if ONE charge was not dropped, I still would have to go to prison for a minimum of 4½ years.

17 Felony Charges: NOT GUILTY

STATE OF NORTH CAROLINA In the General Court of Justice Superior Court Division ____EDGECOMBE____ County	File No. **13CR 02058** Film No.
STATE VERSUS DEFENDANT PRISCILLA EVERETTE-OATES	INDICTMENT

I.   EMBEZZLEMENT BY LOCAL OFFICER OR EMPLOYEE

The jurors for the State upon their oath present that on or about the 6ᵗʰ day of August, 2010, up to and including 25ᵗʰ day of August, 2010, in the county named above the defendant named above unlawfully, willfully and feloniously did embezzle and corruptly use and misapply $372.02, property belonging to the Town of Princeville, by charging that amount on credit card number XXXX-XXXX-XXXX-XXXX-1926, a credit card issued to the Town of Princeville, and incurring those charges and fees. At the time the defendant held the position of Mayor of the Town of Princeville, as an officer of that town, and in that capacity had been entrusted with the property described above. This act is in violation of G.S. 14-92.

II.   EMBEZZLEMENT BY LOCAL OFFICER OR EMPLOYEE

And the jurors for the State upon their oath present that on or about the 10ᵗʰ day of September, 2010, up to and including the 24ᵗʰ day of September, 2010, in the county named above the defendant named above unlawfully, willfully and feloniously did embezzle and corruptly use and misapply $364.46, property belonging to the Town of Princeville, by charging that amount on credit card number XXXX-XXXX-XXXX-1926, a credit card issued to the Town of Princeville, and incurring those charges and fees. At the time the defendant held the position of Mayor of the Town of Princeville, as an officer of that town, and in that capacity had been entrusted with the property described above. This act is in violation of G.S. 14-92.

III.   EMBEZZLEMENT BY LOCAL OFFICER OR EMPLOYEE

And the jurors for the State upon their oath present that on or about the 5ᵗʰ day of October, 2010, up to and including the 27ᵗʰ day of October, 2010, in the county named above the defendant named above unlawfully, willfully and feloniously did embezzle and corruptly use and misapply $429.13, property belonging to the Town of Princeville, by charging that amount on credit card number XXXX-XXXX-XXXX-1926, a credit card issued to the Town of Princeville, and incurring those charges and fees. At the time the defendant held the position of Mayor of the Town of Princeville, as an officer of that town, and in that capacity had been entrusted with the property described above. This act is in violation of G.S. 14-92.

IV.   EMBEZZLEMENT BY LOCAL OFFICER OR EMPLOYEE

And the jurors for the State upon their oath present that on or about the 2ⁿᵈ day of November, 2010, up to and including the 24ᵗʰ day of November, 2010, in the county named above the defendant named above unlawfully, willfully and feloniously did embezzle and corruptly use and misapply $444.73, property belonging to the Town of Princeville, by charging that amount on credit card number XXXX-XXXX-XXXX-1926, a credit card issued to the Town of Princeville, and incurring those charges and fees. At the time the defendant held the position of Mayor of the Town of Princeville, as an officer of that town, and in that capacity had been entrusted with the property described above. This act is in violation of G.S. 14-92.

V.   EMBEZZLEMENT BY LOCAL OFFICER OR EMPLOYEE

And the jurors for the State upon their oath present that on or about the 3ʳᵈ day of December, 2010, up to and including the 21ˢᵗ day of December, 2010, in the county named above the defendant named above unlawfully, willfully and feloniously did embezzle

.and corruptly use and misapply $239.55, property belonging to the Town of Princeville, by charging that amount on credit card number XXXX-XXXX-XXXX-1926, a credit card issued to the Town of Princeville, and incurring those charges and fees. At the time the defendant held the position of Mayor of the Town of Princeville, as an officer of that town, and in that capacity had been entrusted with the property described above. This act is in violation of G.S. 14-92.

VI.   EMBEZZLEMENT BY LOCAL OFFICER OR EMPLOYEE

And the jurors for the State upon their oath present that on or about the 7th day of January, 2011, up to and including the 30th day of January, 2011, in the county named above the defendant named above unlawfully, willfully and feloniously did embezzle and corruptly use and misapply $406.74, property belonging to the Town of Princeville, by charging that amount on credit card number XXXX-XXXX-XXXX-1926, a credit card issued to the Town of Princeville, and incurring those charges and fees. At the time the defendant held the position of Mayor of the Town of Princeville, as an officer of that town, and in that capacity had been entrusted with the property described above. This act is in violation of G.S. 14-92.

VII.   EMBEZZLEMENT BY LOCAL OFFICER OR EMPLOYEE

And the jurors for the State upon their oath present that on or about the 12th day of February, 2011, up to and including the 26th day of February, 2011, in the county named above the defendant named above unlawfully, willfully and feloniously did embezzle and corruptly use and misapply $334.56, property belonging to the Town of Princeville, by charging that amount on credit card number XXXX-XXXX-XXXX-1926, a credit card issued to the Town of Princeville, and incurring those charges and fees. At the time the defendant held the position of Mayor of the Town of Princeville, as an officer of that town, and in that capacity had been entrusted with the property described above. This act is in violation of G.S. 14-92.

VIII.   EMBEZZLEMENT BY LOCAL OFFICER OR EMPLOYEE

And the jurors for the State upon their oath present that on or about the 3rd day of March, 2011, up to an including the 25th day of March, 2011, in the county named above the defendant named above unlawfully, willfully and feloniously did embezzle and corruptly use and misapply $152.73, property belonging to the Town of Princeville, by charging that amount on credit card number XXXX-XXXX-XXXX-1926, a credit card issued to the Town of Princeville, and incurring those charges and fees. At the time the defendant held the position of Mayor of the Town of Princeville, as an officer of that town, and in that capacity had been entrusted with the property described above. This act is in violation of G.S. 14-92.

IX.   EMBEZZLEMENT BY LOCAL OFFICER OR EMPLOYEE

And the jurors for the State upon their oath present that on or about the 1st day of April, 2011, up to and including the 25th day of April, 2011, in the county named above the defendant named above unlawfully, willfully and feloniously did embezzle and corruptly use and misapply $395.43, property belonging to the Town of Princeville, by charging that amount on credit card number XXXX-XXXX-XXXX-1926, a credit card issued to the Town of Princeville, and incurring those charges and fees. At the time the defendant held the position of Mayor of the Town of Princeville, as an officer of that town, and in that capacity had been entrusted with the property described above. This act is in violation of G.S. 14-92.

X.   EMBEZZLEMENT BY LOCAL OFFICER OR EMPLOYEE

And the jurors for the State upon their oath present that on or about the 9th day of May, 2011, up to and including the 25th day of May, 2011, in the county named above the defendant named above unlawfully, willfully and feloniously did embezzle and corruptly use and misapply $290.46, property belonging to the Town of Princeville, by charging that amount on credit card number XXXX-XXXX-XXXX-1926, a credit card issued to the Town of Princeville, and incurring those charges and fees. At the time the defendant held the position of Mayor of the Town of Princeville, as an officer of that town, and in that capacity had been entrusted with the property described above. This act is in violation of G.S. 14-92.

XI.   EMBEZZLEMENT BY LOCAL OFFICER OR EMPLOYEE

And the jurors for the State upon their oath present that on or about the 1st day of June, 2011, up to and including the 29th day of June, 2011, in the county named above the defendant named above unlawfully, willfully and feloniously did embezzle and corruptly use and misapply $416.09, property belonging to the Town of Princeville, by charging that amount on credit card number XXXX-XXXX-XXXX-1926, a credit card issued to the Town of Princeville, and incurring those charges and fees. At the time the defendant held the position of Mayor of the Town of Princeville, as an officer of that town, and in that capacity had been entrusted with the property described above. This act is in violation of G.S. 14-92.

XII.   EMBEZZLEMENT BY LOCAL OFFICER OR EMPLOYEE

17 Felony Charges: NOT GUILTY

And the jurors for the State upon their oath present that on or about the 6th day of July, 2011, up to and including the 22nd day of July, 2011, in the county named above the defendant named above unlawfully, willfully and feloniously did embezzle and corruptly use and misapply $523.66, property belonging to the Town of Princeville, by charging that amount on credit card number XXXX-XXXX-XXXX-1926, a credit card issued to the Town of Princeville, and incurring those charges and fees. At the time the defendant held the position of Mayor of the Town of Princeville, as an officer of that town, and in that capacity had been entrusted with the property described above. This act is in violation of G.S. 14-92.

XIII. EMBEZZLEMENT BY LOCAL OFFICER OR EMPLOYEE

And the jurors for the State upon their oath present that on or about the 15th day of August, 2011, in the county named above the defendant named above unlawfully, willfully and feloniously did embezzle and corruptly use and misapply $98.92, property belonging to the Town of Princeville, by charging that amount on credit card number XXXX-XXXX-XXXX-1926, a credit card issued to the Town of Princeville, and incurring those charges and fees. At the time the defendant held the position of Mayor of the Town of Princeville, as an officer of that town, and in that capacity had been entrusted with the property described above. This act is in violation of G.S. 14-92.

XIV. EMBEZZLEMENT BY LOCAL OFFICER OR EMPLOYEE

And the jurors for the State upon their oath present that on or about the 1st day of September, 2011, up to and including the 23rd day of September, 2011, in the county named above the defendant named above unlawfully, willfully and feloniously did embezzle and corruptly use and misapply $399.34, property belonging to the Town of Princeville, by charging that amount on credit card number XXXX-XXXX-XXXX-1926, a credit card issued to the Town of Princeville, and incurring those charges and fees. At the time the defendant held the position of Mayor of the Town of Princeville, as an officer of that town, and in that capacity had been entrusted with the property described above. This act is in violation of G.S. 14-92.

XV. EMBEZZLEMENT BY LOCAL OFFICER OR EMPLOYEE

And the jurors for the State upon their oath present that on or about the 28th day of October, 2011, up to and including the 31st day of October, 2011, in the county named above the defendant named above unlawfully, willfully and feloniously did embezzle and corruptly use and misapply $161.70, property belonging to the Town of Princeville, by charging that amount on credit card number XXXX-XXXX-XXXX-1926, a credit card issued to the Town of Princeville, and incurring those charges and fees. At the time the defendant held the position of Mayor of the Town of Princeville, as an officer of that town, and in that capacity had been entrusted with the property described above. This act is in violation of G.S. 14-92.

XVI. EMBEZZLEMENT BY LOCAL OFFICER OR EMPLOYEE

And the jurors for the State upon their oath present that on or about the 2nd day of November, 2011 up to and including the 29th day of November, 2011, in the county named above the defendant named above unlawfully, willfully and feloniously did embezzle and corruptly use and misapply $530.21, property belonging to the Town of Princeville, by charging that amount on credit card number XXXX-XXXX-XXXX-1926, a credit card issued to the Town of Princeville, and incurring those charges and fees. At the time the defendant held the position of Mayor of the Town of Princeville, as an officer of that town, and in that capacity had been entrusted with the property described above. This act is in violation of G.S. 14-92.

Priscilla E. Oates

XVII. EMBEZZLEMENT BY LOCAL OFFICER OR EMPLOYEE

And the jurors for the State upon their oath present that on or about the 7th day of January, 2012, up to and including the 25th day of January, 2012, in the county named above the defendant named above unlawfully, willfully and feloniously did embezzle and corruptly use and misapply $74.21, property belonging to the Town of Princeville, by charging that amount on credit card number XXXX-XXXX-XXXX-1926, a credit card issued to the Town of Princeville, and incurring those charges and fees. At the time the defendant held the position of Mayor of the Town of Princeville, as an officer of that town, and in that capacity had been entrusted with the property described above. This act is in violation of G.S. 14-92.

Signature of Prosecutor

WITNESSES		
☒ Agent L. Chapman, NCSBI	☐	Barry Long, NC State Auditor's Office
☐	☐	
☐	☐	

The witnesses marked "X" were sworn by the undersigned Foreman of the Grand Jury and, after hearing testimony, this bill was found to be:

☒ A TRUE BILL by twelve or more grand jurors, and I the undersigned Foreman of the Grand Jury, attest the concurrence of twelve or more grand jurors in this Bill of indictment.

☐ NOT A TRUE BILL

Date 8-5-13   Signature of Grand Jury Foreman

17 Felony Charges: NOT GUILTY

STATE OF NORTH CAROLINA

File No. ▸ ~~12-CRS-003050~~

EDGECOMBE _____ County

In The General Court Of Justice
Superior Court Division

STATE VERSUS

Name And Address Of Defendant
EVERETTE-OATES,PRISCILLA
~~███████████████~~

PRINCEVILLE   NC   27886

NOTICE OF RETURN OF
BILL OF INDICTMENT

G.S. 15A-630, 15A-941(d)

To The Defendant Named Above:

Take notice that the grand jury of the county named above has returned the attached True Bill(s) of Indictment charging you with the offense(s) specified.

You are informed that there are important time limitations on your right to discovery of the evidence against you. (See G.S. 15A-902, which is printed on the reverse.)

This Notice is issued upon the order of the presiding judge.

You will be arraigned on the charges contained in this Indictment only if you file a written request for arraignment with the Clerk of Superior Court not later than twenty-one (21) days after the Indictment is served on you. If you do not file a written request for arraignment within that time, the court will enter a not guilty plea on your behalf.

You must appear in Superior Court at the date, time and place shown below to answer the charges in this Indictment.
NOTE: _If an earlier court date is set in a release order, you must appear at that time also._

Date Of Hearing	Time Of Hearing	Place Of Hearing
8/7/13	9:30 ☑ AM ☐ PM	Tarboro Superior Court

NOTE: _Attach True Bill(s) of Indictment and a copy of the Order of Arrest, if appropriate._

Date Issued
08/05/13

Signature
Kimbery H. Hamel

☐ Deputy CSC   ☑ Assistant CSC   ☐ Clerk Of Superior Court

CERTIFICATE OF NOTICE

I certify that I issued a copy of this Notice to the defendant named above at the address shown by:

☐ 1. Mailing it through the U.S. Postal Service.

☑ 2. Attaching it to an Order for Arrest to be served on the defendant.

☐ 3. Other: (specify)

Date
8/7/13

Signature
Kimb. H. Haw

☐ Deputy CSC   ☑ Assistant CSC   ☐ Clerk Of Superior Court

AOC-CR-216, Rev. 10/04
© 2004 Administrative Office of the Courts

Original-File   Copy-Defendant
(Over)

DA000006

172

Priscilla E. Oates

STATE OF NORTH CAROLINA	File No. 13CRS

EDGECOMBE County

<table>
<tr><td>STATE OF NORTH CAROLINA</td><td>In The General Court Of Justice
☐ District   ☒ Superior Court Division</td></tr>
</table>

	Additional File Numbers
VERSUS	
PRISCILLA EVERETTE-OATES	**SUBPOENA**
	G.S. 1A-1, Rule 45; G.S. 8-59

Party Requesting Subpoena	NOTE TO PARTIES NOT REPRESENTED BY COUNSEL: *Subpoenas may be produced at your request, but*
☒ State/Plaintiff ☐ Defendant	*must be signed and issued by the office of the Clerk of Superior Court, or by a magistrate or judge.*

TO
Name And Address Of Person Subpoenaed	Alternate Address
AGENT L. B. CHAPMAN 1013 W.H. SMITH BLVD. GREENVILLE, NC 27834	

Telephone No. 252-756-4755	Telephone No.

YOU ARE COMMANDED TO: (check all that apply):

☒ appear and testify, in the above entitled action, before the court at the place, date and time indicated below.

☐ appear and testify, in the above entitled action, at a deposition at the place, date and time indicated below.

☐ produce and permit inspection and copying of the following items, at the place, date and time indicated below.

    ☐ See attached list. (List here if space sufficient)

Name And Location Of Court/Place Of Deposition/Place To Produce	Date To Appear/Produce
EDGECOMBE COUNTY GRAND JURY	08/05/2013
EDGECOMBE CO. COURTHOUSE, 301 ST. ANDREWS ST.	Time To Appear/Produce 10:00 ☒ AM ☐ PM
TARBORO, NC 27886	

Name And Address Of Applicant Or Applicant's Attorney	Date 07/10/2013
TONYA OLIVER MONTANYE, FCP P.O. BOX 1468 NEW BERN, NC 28563	Signature

Telephone No. Of Applicant Or Applicant's Attorney 252-639-3133	☐ Deputy CSC ☐ Magistrate	☐ Assistant CSC ☒ Attorney/DA	☐ Clerk Of Superior Court ☐ District Court Judge	☐ Superior Court Judge

RETURN OF SERVICE

I certify this subpoena was received and served on the person subpoenaed as follows:

By ☐ personal delivery.   ☐ registered or certified mail, receipt requested and attached.

☐ telephone communication by Sheriff *(use only for a witness subpoenaed to appear and testify).*

☐ telephone communication by local law enforcement agency *(use only for a witness subpoenaed to appear and testify in a criminal case).*
NOTE TO COURT: *If the witness was served by telephone communication from a local law enforcement agency in a criminal case, the court may not issue a show cause order or order for arrest against the witness until the witness has been served personally with the written subpoena.*

☐ I was unable to serve this subpoena. Reason unable to serve: _____

Service Fee $	☐ Paid ☐ Due	Date Served	Name Of Authorized Server (Type Or Print)	Signature Of Authorized Server	Title

NOTE TO PERSON REQUESTING SUBPOENA: *A copy of this subpoena must be delivered, mailed or faxed to the attorney for each party in this case. If a party is not represented by an attorney, the copy must be mailed or delivered to the party. This does not apply in criminal cases.*

AOC-G-100, Rev. 5/13
© 2013 Administrative Office of the Courts

(Please See Reverse Side)

DA000954

173

17 Felony Charges: NOT GUILTY

After I was indicted, I made a public response on WHIG-TV on August 26, 2013 stating I was innocent of the charges placed upon me.

You may scan the QR code to watch the video in its entirety.

SCAN HERE

Agent Chapman was sent to DOJ (Department of Justice) to the Medicaid Fraud Dept to falsely investigate my private business.

Atty Bonner corresponded via email with the Assistant Atty General Medicaid Investigations Division and confirmed that Agent Chapman refused to follow requests on obtaining documents.

Hello Ms. Bing,

Hope all is well with you and you are enjoying the waning of Spring.

As you know, SBI Agent L. B. Chapman is at present copying the records at my client's business, ** LLC.

Ms. Chapman and her staff are removing stapled documents and are refusing to re-staple the documents and return the records to the condition and order in which they were found.

This is a violation of the Request for Records Document (Attached) Ms. Chapman and Ms. Oates signed on May 5, 2014.

Specifically, the signed REQUEST FOR RECORDS document provides, in pertinent part, the following: *"The investigators will make every efforts to conduct this review during normal business hours, to minimize interference with your ongoing business activities, and to return all records to the condition and order in which they were found."*

Pursuant to my instructions, Ms. Oates asked Agent Chapman to sign a statement acknowledging receipt of **'s request to comply with the signed REQUEST FOR RECORDS document, stating" "Please, we would like you to leave the files in the exact manner in which we provided them to you, including re-stapling all the documents so that we could protect the clients' confidential HIPAA information." (Also Attached)

Ms. Chapman refused to signed **'s Request and refused to re-staple the files and return the files and "all records in the condition and order in which they were found."

Again, we seek your help and valued insight to assure compliance with Ms. Chapman's written representation "to return all records to the condition and order in which they were found."

Eager to speak with you if needed at your convenience.

Charles

Charles A. Bonner
Law Offices of Bonner & Bonner
475 Gate Five Rd, Suite 212
Sausalito, CA 94965
tel 415-331-3070
fax 415-331-2738
email: charles@bonnerlaw.com

17 Felony Charges: NOT GUILTY

In September 2015, my business was reinstated and LIFTED from the suspension with NO record of fraud!! It was still challenging to get back to normal after all of the things my team and I went through. Think of the shame and embarrassment these corrupt people put us through for no reason! I was mortified, but to God be the glory!

The following document is the "STOP SUSPENSION OF PAYMENTS" from the NC Dept of Health & Human Services Division of Medical Assistance which confirmed the suspension of Medicaid payments would end on September 24, 2015.

Priscilla C. Oates

North Carolina Department of Health and Human Services
Division of Medical Assistance

Pat McCrory
Governor

Richard O. Brajer
Secretary

Dave Richard
Deputy Secretary for Medical Assistance

September 24, 2015

CERTIFIED MAIL
70101060000206665756

~~[REDACTED]~~

Tarboro, NC 27886-1634

<u>PI Case #: 2013-1082</u>

Subject: **Stop Suspension of Payments – Notice to Provider**

Dear Provider:

Pursuant to 42 CFR § 455.23(a), The Division of Medical Assistance (DMA) must suspend payments to a provider when the agency determines a credible allegation of fraud exists for which an investigation is pending. DMA received a credible allegation of fraud against ~~[REDACTED]~~

The allegation included but may not be limited to: an allegation that the provider billed for services not rendered during the period 1/1/11-1/30/13 and constituted the nature of the payment suspension action.

This suspension applied to all Medicaid claims submitted by the provider number(s) listed below and was effective 8/12/14. This letter serves as formal notice of termination of this action.

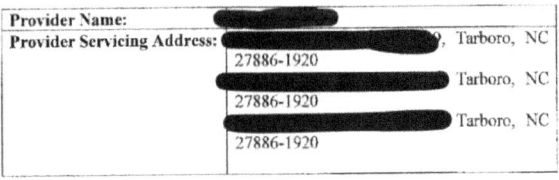

Provider Name:	~~[REDACTED]~~		
Provider Servicing Address:	~~[REDACTED]~~	, Tarboro, NC	27886-1920
	~~[REDACTED]~~	Tarboro, NC	27886-1920
	~~[REDACTED]~~	Tarboro, NC	27886-1920

www.ncdhhs.gov
Tel 919-855-4100 • Fax 919-733-6608
Location: 1985 Umstead Drive • Kirby Building • Raleigh, NC 27603
Mailing Address: 2501 Mail Service Center • Raleigh, NC 27699-2501
An Equal Opportunity / Affirmative Action Employer

Stop Suspension of Payments – Notice to Provider
Version 1.1, revised 8/27/2015

17 Felony Charges: NOT GUILTY

	316 Russell Drive, Princeville, NC 27886-9542
Locator Code:	003, 004, 005, 006, 007
PI Case Number:	2013-1082
Legacy Provider Number:	8303306, 8301751
NPI:	1336291699
Taxonomy:	251S00000X Community/Behavioral Health

The payment suspension is for a temporary period. Pursuant to 42 CFR § 455.23(c), payment suspension will not continue effective 9/24/15 based on:

☒ The agency or the prosecuting authorities determined that there is insufficient evidence of fraud

☐ Legal proceedings related to the alleged fraud are completed.

If you have any questions regarding this notice, please contact me directly at 919-814-0000.

Sincerely,

Patrick Piggott, Section Chief
Behavioral Health Review Section
Program Integrity

pp/mw

cc: Rob Kindsvatter, DMA Director of Compliance
        Pat Delbridge, Program Integrity Administrative Officer
        Sheila Platts, DMA Provider and Recipient Services
        Sandra Terrell, DMA Chief Operations Officer
        Laketha Miller, DHHS Controller
        Belinda Smith, NCDOJ Health and Public Assistance
        LMEs / LME-MCOs
        Medicaid Investigations Division

9.

Attorney Malvern King

Atty King was one of my NC lawyers who worked with the other attorneys to get my businesses back up and running after Lolita Chapman shut them down. When she was placed in the Medicaid fraud department, the very first business she came after were my private businesses, though her focus should have been on the town of Princeville.

It was Malvern King who represented me and cleared my businesses. Unfortunately, we received no income for 14 months as a result of the fraudulent allegations until the suspension was lifted.

As a result of the suspension, we were not able to pay bills or conduct business as usual. It was completely devastating! You can go back to Chapter 8, pg 177-178 to read the **Suspension Lifted Notice** that confirms the suspension was lifted.

The MCO did not want to restore my business and Atty King had to write a letter to the DMA requesting for my business to be restored back to its full operating position, and for the MCO to make payment for all services rendered by my business. Below are corresponding emails:

17 Felony Charges: NOT GUILTY

From: Campbell, Thomas [mailto:TCampbell@ncdoj.gov]
Sent: Monday, October 12, 2015 10:02 AM
To: Malvern King
Subject: ___ v. DHHS 14 DHR 09286, PI 2013-1082

Mal:

I've spoken with DMA regarding the issues that we discussed in our last call. The MCO has been notified by DMA that the suspension was lifted. Additionally, as I expected, the MCO is the entity that your client needs to talk to about any payments that may have been withheld due to the suspension. DMA does not handle the payments to providers for specific claims, so it doesn't have this information.

Please let me know what your client finds out about any pending payments and when you will be able to file the Voluntary Dismissal.

Thank you.

Tom

Thomas J. Campbell
Assistant Attorney General
Public Assistance Section
N.C. Department of Justice
P.O. Box 629
Raleigh, NC 27602-0629
Telephone: (919) 716-6845
Fax: (919) 716-6758

Priscilla E. Oates

From: Harris, Atwar P [mailto:patrice.harris@dhhs.nc.gov]
Sent: Friday, August 29, 2014 11:09 AM
To: Malvern King
Subject: RE: ___, LLC Program Integrity Case#: 2013-1082

Good morning Attorney King – I received the voicemail message you left at my office this morning and the below email message regarding the schedule conflict during the week of September 8-12. Please advise of the availability of all interested parties for an alternate hearing date of September 16 or 17 at 1:30 p.m. Please also advise of Mrs. Oates' full name and title.

Thank you in advance and I look forward to hearing from you.

A. Patrice Harris, J.D., M.P.P.
N.C. Department of Health and Human Services
Hearing Officer
333 East Six Forks Road
Raleigh, NC 27609
Phone: (919) 814-0090
Fax: (919) 814-0032
patrice.harris@dhhs.nc.gov
www.ncdhhs.gov

17 Felony Charges: NOT GUILTY

From: Malvern King [mailto:MFK@pwkl.com]
Sent: Friday, August 29, 2014 10:36 AM
To: Harris, Atwar P
Subject: RE: _____, LLC Program Integrity Case#: 2013-1082

Hearing Officer Harris:

   Thank you for your email concerning the setting of the Hearing for the subject case. The week of Sept 8-12 may be problematic for ___, LLC. Due to a conflict for me and for Mrs. Oates. If you are able to do so, could you call me today before 12 Noon or next Tuesday, Sept 2 at 919-682-9691. Thank you.

v/r Malvern King

From: Harris, Atwar P [mailto:patrice.harris@dhhs.nc.gov]
Sent: Thursday, August 28, 2014 3:48 PM
To: Malvern King
Subject: ___, LLC Program Integrity Case#: 2013-1082

Good afternoon – I will conduct the reconsideration review hearing requested by ___, LLC. I received the August 27, 2014 letter from your office giving notice that your firm will represent _____, LLC in this matter.

On August 25, 2014, ___, LLC requested an in-person review hearing of the August 4, 2014 decision by the N.C. Department of Health and Human Services – Division of Medical Assistance (DMA) to suspend payments to ___, LLC under the Medicaid program pursuant to 42 CFR §455.23(a).

The proposed review dates and times are: September 10, 2014 at 1:30 p.m. or September 11, 2014 at 1:30 p.m. Please advise regarding the availability of all interested parties. Please also advise of name, title, and number of provider representatives who will attend the hearing.

If you wish to submit additional documentation to the Hearing Office in support of your client's appeal, you may do so to my attention at the below mailing address. The documentation will be forwarded to the DMA Program Integrity representative for their review.

Thank you in advance and I look forward to hearing from you.

A. Patrice Harris, J.D., M.P.P.
N.C. Department of Health and Human Services
Hearing Officer
333 East Six Forks Road
Raleigh, NC 27609
Phone: (919) 814-0090
Fax: (919) 814-0032
patrice.harris@dhhs.nc.gov
www.ncdhhs.gov

Atty King also confirmed that there was an economic development committee during my administration. During his deposition, he talked about the visions and goals I had for the town of Princeville and how we wanted to bring business to the town for revenue and employment for Princeville residents.

On the following pages are a portion of Atty King's deposition.

17 Felony Charges: NOT GUILTY

Here is the QR code for you to scan with your phone if you would like to read the deposition in its entirety.

Priscilla E. Oates

1   proceeding, but I do not--I did not know exactly

2   when that began so--

3   Q   All right. Very good. If you go down to the

    bottom of that paragraph, she says "I also met with

4

    and interviewed former Princeville mayor Delia

5

    Perkins." Do you see where I'm reading?

6

7   A   Yes.

8   Q   Okay. "Like Ms. Harris, Ms. Perkins had not been

    interviewed previously by the SBI. Ms. Perkins

9

    advised that she was the mayor who directly

10

    preceded Mayor Everette-Oates. Ms. Perkins advised

11

    that she had an economic development committee but

12

    never took trips out of--out of the Town of

13

    Princeville for meetings. She advised that this

14

    was not a formal committee in the sense that the

15

    town council had created the committee but was an

16

    executive committee and that the mayor is allowed

17

    to have executive committees. Again, Agent Chapman

18

    was present for this interview in which Ms. Perkins

19

    shared this information."

20

            And while you were representing Mayor

21

    Oates, you were aware that she had formed an

22

    executive committee and that was to bring economic

23

    development to her Town of Princeville?

24

17 Felony Charges: NOT GUILTY

1   MS. HILL: Objection.

2   MR. LINDSLEY: Objection.

3   MR. RABINOVITZ: Objection. Leading.

4   And I will also note for the record that as is

5   permitted to us under the rules, we will be asking

6   that either this entire document be published to

7   the jury or that you read it without skipping over

8   parts of the document.

9   MR. BONNER: Oh, yes. Most definitely we

10   will publish the entire document. Ms. Montanye

11   will testify to it. She's already been deposed.

12   But most definitely.

13   MR. RABINOVITZ: Very good.

14   MR. BONNER: It's a stipulation that the

15   entire document will go to the jury. We all

16   stipulate to that. So stipulate?

17   MR. RABINOVITZ: No. We may make an

18   objection to it on other grounds. But to the

19   extent that it--to the extent that you are allowed

20   to read parts of it to the jury, we may make an

21   appropriate motion that the entire document be--

22   MR. BONNER: Certainly.

23   MR. RABINOVITZ: --published to the jury.

24   MR. BONNER: Certainly.

1		MR. RABINOVITZ: We're--we're not
2		stipulating to anything right now.
3		MR. LINDSLEY: Nor is Beth Wood.
4		MS. HILL: Nor Agent Chapman.
5	Q	Did you want to say something, sir?
6	A	Go ahead and ask me.
7	Q	Okay. Very good. My question was that you were
8		aware that Mayor Oates had an economic development
9		committee?
10	A	I was aware that Mayor Oates had a committee, yes.
11		I would call it an economic development committee.
12		I don't recall that it had that name but that--
13	Q	Yes.
14	A	Let me just add if I may in responding to that that
15		Mayor Oates was--was mayor of Princeville before
16		Delia Perkins for--for--for a term. And then Ms.
17		Perkins was mayor, and then Mayor Oates became
18		mayor again. And Mayor Oates advised me in one of
19		our conversations that she--she was very concerned
20		about bringing business into Princeville, that
21		Princeville is a very poor community and has
22		suffered a lot of damage from floods. It is very
23		low. It's adjacent to Tarboro on the Tar River,
24		and the town has been flooded on numerous

Page 10

187

17 Felony Charges: NOT GUILTY

1   occasions. And she had worked very hard in her

2   prior term as mayor to--to bring businesses and in

3   fact brought some businesses into town--into the

4   Town of Princeville--I don't recall the names of

5   them right now--but to provide employment for--for

6   Princeville residents. And so this was a concern

7   of hers which she carried from that term into--into

8   the current term.

9 Q   Does it refresh your recollection that she brought

10   in a health center--a healthcare center?

11 A   I believe that's correct. Yes.

12 Q   And also she brought in I believe a dollar store?

13 A   That's correct.

14   MR. RABINOVITZ: Objection. Leading.

15 Q   And does it refresh your recollection she also

16   brought in I believe a scrap metal company?

17   MR. RABINOVITZ: Objection.

18 A   I'm not sure about names.

19 Q   But that was consistent with your understanding of

20   her efforts to provide economic development to this

21   otherwise economically depressed town itself?

22 A   Yes.

23 Q   Okay. Going to page--top of Page 3, she writes--

24   Ms. Montanye--DA Montanye writes, quote, "I also

Page 10

1   met with Robin Hammond, Vance Holloman and Sharon

2   Edmundson to prepare for the trial in August of

3   2014. Agent Chapman was also present. During this

4   meeting which was held in the LGC conference room

5   on the second floor, Sharon Edmundson advised that

6   I should make contact with Phyllis Pearson, a

7   certified public accounting firm in Zebulon, who

8   had performed the town audit which essentially

9   triggered this investigation as it contained

10   negative or adverse findings."

11   Is it your understanding that Ms. Hammond

12   was the attorney for the LGC?

13   A   Yes. I did know that.

14   Q   And Mr. Holloman was the--he was the director of

15   the deputy treasurer?

16   A   That's what I understand, yes.

17   Q   And Ms. Sharon Edmundson was the CPA for the LGC?

18   A   Yes. Yes.

19   Q   Going to the next sentence, it says, quote, "Ms.

20   Pearson had never been interviewed by the SBI. Ms.

21   Edmundson also advised me that they were not aware

22   of who had created a spreadsheet that had been used

23   during the investigation of this matter," period.

24   Now, in your interaction with Ms.

17 Felony Charges: NOT GUILTY

10.

Affidavits & Declarations

On the following pages you will see first-hand accounts of the individuals who testified on my behalf:

Joey T. Petway – Chief of Police, Princeville Police Dept.

Town of Princeville

Mayor Priscilla Everette-Oates

Mayor Pro-Tem Isabelle Purvis-Andrews (Ward 3)
Commissioner Ann B. Howel (Ward 2)

Commissioner Gwendolyn Knight (Ward 1)
Commissioner Calvin Sherrod (Ward 4)

18 September 2013

The Honorable
Priscilla Everette-Oates, Mayor
Town of Princeville
201 South Main Street
Princeville North Carolina 27886

Dear Mayor Oates:

Per your request I am providing this report. During the time that Mr. Victor Marrow was the Town Manager I attended five meetings In reference to economic development for the Town of Princeville. I was asked to attend these meeting by Mr. Victor Marrow.

One of these meeting was held in Greenville NC at the Hilton Hotel month of January 2011. At this meeting were Mayor Oates, Commissioner Sherrod, Commissioner Purvis-Andrews and Mr. Marrow. A presentation was given by Reginald Smith about Comprehensive Economic Develop of the Town of Princeville. In this meeting I was asked about needs and concerns for growth of the Police Department.

Second meeting on or about April 5, 2011, I was asked to attend was at Madison Seafood in Rocky Mount NC. At this meeting were Mayor Oates, Commissioner Purvis-Andrews, Attorney Chuck Watts and Mr. Marrow. Information and brainstorming about Town of Princeville development was discussed.

Third meeting on or about February 16, 2011 was at Stacks Restaurant in Tarboro NC. I was asked to attend by Mr. Marrow and Mayor Oates was present. Representatives from Department of Commerce were present and discussed comprehensive economic development.

Page 1

519

191

17 Felony Charges: NOT GUILTY

The fourth meeting was a survival day event which occurred November 16-18 2011. During this event a career day was held at town hall and followed up by a two day summit at Edgecombe Community College. During this summit Federal, State and Local representatives attended to support economic development for the Town of Princeville. Representatives from USDA, Commerce Department, Governors Office, State Senate and Local elected Official attended this summit. At this meeting I attended at the request of Mr. Victor Marrow and preformed several duties and attended some of the workshops.

This workshop appeared to be a successful and was very informative. Presentations given were excellent.

Page 2

Respectfully submitted

Joey T. Petway
Chief of Police

Oldest Town Chartered By Blacks in America*
Incorporated February 20, 1885
Post Office Box 1527 Tarboro, NC 27886
Telephone: 252-823-1057 Fax. 252-823-5366

520

192

INCIDENT/INVESTIGATION REPORT

Agency Name	Princeville Police Department
ORI	NC 0330500
OCA	12-0167

Date / Time Reported: 09 28 2012 1550 Hrs

INCIDENT DATA

#1 Crime / Incident: Computer Files-Missing/Hacked — ☑ Complete
At Found: 09 27 2012 1700 Hrs
Last Known Secure: 09 27 2012 1600 Hrs

#2 PNC Documents Files Missing — ☑ Complete
Location of Incident: 201 S. Main St. Princeville NC 27886

#3 Personnel Files Missing — ☑ Complete
Premise Type: Town Hall

Victim Residence Type: ☐ Single Family ☐ Mult. Famil.

MO

How Attacked or Committed: Used honet and system and removed files from computer office
Forcible: ☐ Yes ☑ No
Entry: Stain
Weapon / Tools: Honet

Injury: ☐ None ☐ Minor ☐ Loss of Teeth ☐ Broken Bones ☐ Severe Lacerations ☐ Internal ☐ Unconscious ☐ Other Major
Drug/Alcohol Use: ☐ Yes ☐ Unknown ☐ No ☑ N/A

VICTIM

V1 Victim/Business Name (Last, First, Middle): Town of Princeville
Home Address: 201 S. Main St. Princeville NC 27886
Home Phone: 252-823-1057
Business Phone:

VYR	Make	Model	Style	Color	Lic/Lis	VIN

OTHERS INVOLVED

CODES: V=Victim (Denote V2, V3) O=Owner (if other than victim) R=Reporting Person (if other than victim)
Type: ☐ Person ☐ Business ☐ Society ☐ Government ☐ Financial Institute ☐ Religious ☐ L.E. Officer Line of Duty ☐ Other/Unknown

Code R — Name (Last, First, Middle): Boyd, Maggie
DOB / Age: 11-12-1959 72
Race: B Sex: F
Home Address:
Employer Name/Address: 201 S. Main St. Princeville NC 27886
Business Phone: 252-823-1057

PROPERTY

Status Codes: L=Lost S=Stolen R=Recovered D=Damaged Z=Seized B=Burned C=Counterfeit/Forged F=Found

Victim #	DCI	Status	Value	D/I	QTY	Property Description	Make/Model	Serial Number

STATUS

Number of Vehicles Stolen: 0
Number Vehicles Recovered: 0

Officer Name: J.F. Petway   ID#: 1500
Officer Signature:
Supervisor Signature:

Complainant Signature:

Case Status: ☑ Further Investigation ☐ Inactive ☐ Closed/Cleared ☐ Closed/Leads Exhausted

Case Disposition: ☐ Founded ☐ Cleared by Arrest ☐ Cleared by Arrest by Another Agency ☐ Death of Offender ☐ Juvenile/No Custody ☐ Refuse to Cooperate ☐ Prosecution Declined ☐ Extradition Declined

Page ___ of ___

531

17 Felony Charges: NOT GUILTY

Maggie Boyd – interim Princeville Town Mgr

AFFIDAVIT AND DECLARATION

I, Maggie W. Boyd, declare as follows:

1. This Affidavit and Declaration is submitted voluntarily and of my own free will. I have personal knowledge of all facts set forth below and if called to testify, I could and would testify competently to these facts.

2. I am a citizen of Princeville and served as a Board Commissioner in Ward 1 from 2004 until 2007, served as Curator of the Princeville Welcome Center from approximately April 2010 until February 8, 2012, and as Interim Town Manager from February 8, 2012 until March 2013.

3. Attached hereto is my notarized Affidavit dated September 29th, 2012, which is incorporated herein by this reference as though fully set forth in this declaration. I further state that the matters stated in that Affidavit are true and correct. That Affidavit, consisting of two pages, is attached as EXHIBIT 1 to this declaration.

4. On several occasions during August 2012, I observed the financial files of the Town of Princeville spread throughout the board room and the conference room of the Princeville town hall and left unattended for long periods of time.

5. From July 31, 2012, until LGC removed all the files from the premises of the Princeville town hall, sometime in September 2012, I observed Sharon Edmondson and Amy Szalaj, employees of LGC, standing in the main office of the Princeville Town Hall, holding various Princeville original files and folders, preparing to take them to Raleigh with them. As the current Town Manager, I inquired where they were taking these files, and they responded that these were work files of theirs. They proceeded to remove the Town

DECLARATION OF MAGGIE BOYD - 1

581

Priscilla E. Oates

1   original files without authorization or documentation and without signing them out. I

2   never observed them returning any of the original files to Princeville Town Hall.

3   6. I have reviewed and read the 17 charges against Mayor Oates. While I did not personally

4   attend many of the meetings, I did definitely attend a meeting at the Holiday Inn in

5   Rocky Mount in February 2012 and an LGC meeting in July 2012. There were others

6   meetings that I was informed about. Based on my personal knowledge of expenses

7   incurred for a hotel conference room, snacks, gas and incidentals, each of the expenses

8   outlined in each of the 17 charges were customary and necessary charges for the benefit

9   of the town of Princeville during the very necessary planning of the economic

10 development for the town. My town of Princeville is economically depressed and in dire

11 need of economic development. It stemmed from this need that we developed the

12 economic development plan.

13 7. I was fully aware that the meetings were happening and I was specifically informed by

14 Town Manager Victor Marrow about any meetings that dealt with the museum projects in

15 the following ways: through the Mayor's flyers; through the website that the Mayor and

16 the Economic Development Committee developed to keep the citizens informed; through

17 the Town Board meetings; I saw plans from a consultant, Reginald Smith, to help with

18 the economic development plans and the producing of it; the planning for the historic

19 river path, plans for an amphitheater, as well as a 4 x 5 foot billboard at the museum

20 depicting the economic vision plans and progress reports which document that Mayor

21 Oates and her Committee had a vision for Princeville. A true and correct copy of a

22 progress report dated December 20, 2010, is an example of the progress report (produced

23 by Princeville Economic Development Committee (EXHIBIT 2). I am aware that Mayor

DECLARATION OF MAGGIE BOYD - 2
582

195

1   Oates and Princeville Economic Development Committee worked on the Town's

2   Museum Tourism and Welcome center approximately from January 2011 through April

3   2011; worked on the plans to have a water plant for the Town of Princeville; constantly

4   discussing the economic vision plan and progress reports from August 2010 through

5   November 2013; working on getting grocery stores, a fast food restaurant, post office,

6   and shopping center from November 2010 through July 2011; worked on plans for Small

7   Business and Entrepreneurship in order for our citizens to get jobs. They brought a job

8   fair to Princeville. The Mayor and her Staff helped start a helpline phone call center

9   calling for citizens to call in if they needed help after Hurricane Irene. Shortly afterward,

10   the State declared that the Town was a Disaster area in September 2011. Mayor Oates

11   and Mayor Pro Tem Andrews went from door to door to find out what the citizens needed

12   to survive and what the Town could do to help provide for them. I knew that the Town

13   was faced with disaster because I have lived in Princeville all of my life.

14   8. I became the Interim Town Manager on February 8, 2012. Mayor Oates informed me that

15   I was to be part of the Economic Development Committee Team, since Victor Marrow

16   had quit as town manager (Exhibit 3). I did attend the planning meeting at the Holiday

17   Inn in Rocky Mount on February 2012. I was also aware of many previous planning

18   meetings and necessary expenses for these meetings, most of which were attended by

19   Victor Marrow who then informed me of anything relating to the Princeville Museum

20   and Welcome Center. Victor Marrow, the then Town Manager, had a pattern, practice

21   and custom of discussing with me and informing me of planned economic development

22   meetings, and he had a pattern, practice and custom of reporting to me the content of the

23   meetings, the progress of the planning and the progress of his participation in the

3

DECLARATION OF MAGGIE BOYD - 3

583

planning. The purpose of these discussions with Victor Marrow, both before and after these economic development meetings, was for me to be able to give feedback and new ideas to the Mayor, primarily because of my extensive historical knowledge of the town since my family has been in Princeville since the turn of the century.

9. As examples, I have specifically reviewed charge #6 and an amount of $48.18 for a meal at Madison's Seafood and gas for $40.08, totaling $88.26, reflecting a meeting on January 7, 2011, regarding the museum project and a brochure. Victor Marrow reported to me about this meeting. I do attest that based on my knowledge, these expenses were ordinary, necessary and customary, to benefit the town of Princeville.

10. I am also familiar with charge #7, regarding three meetings in the total amount of $334.56, one in Raleigh on February 12, 2011 concerning a water plant for the town, one at Madison's Seafood in Rocky Mount February 15, 2011, regarding the progress reports, and one regarding grants through local and State agencies at the Holiday Inn in Rocky Mount on February 26, 2011.

11. Another charge I am personally familiar with is charge #8, in the amount of $152.73. These charges were incurred in a meeting in Raleigh on April 1, 2011, attended by Mayor Oates, Mayor pro Tem Isabelle Andrews, Reggie Smith, and Victor Marrow. When Victor Marrow returned to the Town Hall, Victor Marrow reported to me that they had discussed increasing tourism and making the museum more attractive to tourists, establishing a museum display on George Washington Carver. I have personally seen a letter subsequently drafted by Victor Marrow and the Princeville Economic Development Committee on the discussion of the Tuskegee Institute, which was carbon copied to me. (Exhibit 4).

4

1   12. I attended the Princeville Survival Week Conference on November 16 – 18, 2011. It was

2   highly a success with the Local, State, and Federal Representatives being present.

3   13. In this same manner I am familiar with virtually all of the meetings, and with the ordinary

4   and customary expenses arising from those charges, even though I did not personally

5   attended these meetings.

6   14. I have reviewed all the allegations in all counts of the indictment and can and do hereby

7   attest that all of these expenses were used for the benefit of the Town of Princeville and

8   no part of said expenses were embezzled, nor willfully nor corruptly used, nor misapplied

9   for any purpose whatsoever, other than for the purpose for which such funds were held

10   and that such funds were used for the purpose and benefit of the Town of Princeville.

11

12   //

13   //

14   //

15   //

16   //

17   //

18   //

19   //

20   //

21   //

22   //

23   //

24   //

25   //

26

5

198

1 I declare under penalty of perjury under the laws of the State of North Carolina that the

2 foregoing is true, and that this declaration was executed on January 7, 2014, at Rocky

3 Mount, North Carolina.

4

5 MAGGIE W. BOYD

6

7

8

9

10

11

12

13

14

15

16

17

18

19

20

21

22

23

24

25

26

DECLARATION OF MAGGIE BOYD - 6

586

6

17 Felony Charges: NOT GUILTY

AFFIDAVIT

On August 15, 2012, I, Interim Town Manager Maggie Boyd instructed the Former Town Clerk Diana Draughn to review the PNC Bank files to make sure all of the receipts and documents have been filed.

On August 28, 2012, Diana gave me a document that showed me only five (5) receipts were missing from Mayor Oates PNC credit card files.

On September 27, 2012, I was instructed by Mayor Oates to pull the PNC Bank files again for review, due to the fact that Sharon Edmundson (LGC) sent a letter dated September 19, 2012, concerning the PNC Bank files. But, the files were missing from Princeville Town Hall. I asked LGC Staff, Amy Szalaj did she know where the PNC Bank files are. Amy stated that she didn't know. She called and asked Sharon (LGC). Amy gave me eight (8) pages that were faxed from Sharon (LGC). The fax consisted of some of Mayor Oates receipts.

Since the files were still missing, Mayor Oates and I filed a police report on the missing PNC Bank files.

Signature *Maggie M Boyd*

NC, County of Edgecombe
Signed before me on this 27th day
of Sept, 2012 by Maggie M Boyd
Notary Public _Catherine H. ___

My Commission expires: 11/18/17

Daisy Staton – Princeville, NC Town Clerk, Feb-Aug 2012

<u>AFFIDAVIT AND DECLARATION</u>

I, Daisy E. Staton, declare as follows:

1. This Affidavit and Declaration is submitted voluntarily and of my own free will. I have personal knowledge of all facts set forth below and if called to testify, I could and would testify competently to these facts.

2. I am a citizen of Princeville and served as an administrative Town Clerk part-time from February 2012 until August 2012. I also spent many hours volunteering with the Town of Princeville, assisting the former Interim Town Manager, Maggie Boyd. From 2010 until 2013 I served on and was chairperson of the Town of Princeville Planning Board. Currently I serve as chairperson of the Princeville Housing Authority Board.

3. Attached hereto is my notarized Affidavit dated January 7th, 2014, which is incorporated herein by this reference as though fully set forth in this declaration. I further state that the matters stated in that Affidavit are true and correct. That Affidavit is attached as (Exhibit 1) to this declaration.

4. I was made aware by Mayor Oates, through flyers, through the Princeville website through which the Mayor kept citizens informed, at board meetings, and meetings with Mr. Wallace Green and Reginald Smith, as well as a 4 x 5 foot billboard at the museum depicting the economic vision plan and progress reports, that Mayor Oates had a vision for Princeville and the Town had a consultant to help with the economic developments. (See Exhibit 2, a true and correct copy of a progress report dated December 20, 2010, an example of the progress produced by Princeville Economic Development Committee). I am aware that Princeville Economic Development Committee worked on the Town's Museum Tourism and Welcome center approximately from January 2011 through April 2011; worked on the plans to have a water plant for the Town of Princeville; constantly discussing the economic vision plan and progress reports from August 2010 through November 2013; working on getting grocery stores, a fast food restaurant, post office,

DECLARATION OF DAISY STATON - 1

1   and shopping center from November 2010 through July 2011; worked on plans for small

2   business and entrepreneurship to bring jobs for our citizens, as a part of which they

3   brought a job fair to Princeville. After Hurricane Irene the Mayor and the Town Staff

4   started a phone center for people to call for help after the State declared the Town was a

5   Disaster Area in September 2011. Mayor Oates and Mayor Pro Tem Andrews went from

6   door to door to find out what the citizens needed to survive and what the Town could

7   help provide for them (Exhibit 3). Commissioners Ann Howell and Gwendolyn Knight

8   stated it wasn't a disaster, but I knew that the Town was faced with disaster because I live

     in Princeville myself.

9   5.   I was also aware that the Princeville Economic Development Committee held multiple

10   planning meetings at various locations, including hotels and restaurants, trips to

11   Washington D.C. and other locations. I also participated with the mayor in the planning

12   of the Princeville Town Resource Training Summit, which was produced by the

13   Princeville Economic Development Committee. It occurred from November 16 to 18,

14   2011 and was held at the Edgecombe Community College, Tarboro Campus in Tarboro,

15   NC, was well attended, very informative and benefitted me personally through contacts I

16   made. The keynote speaker at the Summit was Dr. Alma Hobbs, Associate Assistant

17   Secretary for Administration at the U.S. Department of Agriculture. By their choice,

18   Commissioners Howell and Knight did not participate in any of the planning or execution

19   of the economic plan but were well aware of the meetings and the progress reports

20   because the planning and the progress reports were well publicized.

21   6.   I am aware that the mayor traveled to the economic planning meetings and I am aware

22   that the mayor incurred expenses for gasoline, meals, hotels and the expenses of

23   producing flyers, materials, handouts and programs. I am also aware that the Mayor sent

24   out flyers with a progress report of her plans in the citizens' water bills almost every

     month, and I received these flyers in my mail. As the Town Administrative Clerk, I

     personally folded some of the flyers and put them with the water bills' envelopes.

25

26

DECLARATION OF DAISY STATON - 2

202

7. I met Mr. Reginald Smith, the consultant through Mayor Oates and the Princeville Economic Development Committee several times. He is a smart man, intelligent and knowledgeable about economic development for cities and municipalities. Not everyone can put together plans and events, and he knew where grants could be found. I met him at least 3 times: at a brainstorming meeting of the Princeville Economic Development Committee at the Holiday Inn in Rocky Mount, February, 2012; the Survivor Week; and the Summit Conference in November 16 through 18, 2011. I am aware that the Mayor and Princeville Economic Development Committee worked on the Princeville Survival week projects started from August 2011 through November 2011. However, as soon as the Princeville Economic Development Committee got to the point of practical execution of the planning, there were many interruptions that were negative, and Local Government Commission (LGC) shut all planning down and took over the financial affairs of Princeville.

8. Mr. Oliver Bass from the North Carolina Commerce Planning Department was appointed by Mr. Henry McKoy to give technical assistance and meet with the Princeville Planning Board once a month. This hard work came out of the efforts of the Economic Development Team of Mayor Oates' Administration.

//
//
//
//
//
//
//
//
//
//
//

DECLARATION OF DAISY STATON - 3

1
2
3
4
5
6
7
8
9
10
11
12
13
14
15
16
17
18
19
20
21
22
23
24
25
26

I declare under penalty of perjury under the laws of the State of North Carolina that the foregoing is true, and that this declaration was executed on January 7, 2014, at Rocky Mount, North Carolina.

Daisy E. Staton
DAISY E. STATON

DECLARATION OF DAISY STATON - 4

Priscilla E. Oates

AFFIDAVIT

I, Daisy Staton, a town clerk do hereby swear and affirm that when LGC took over the financial books of Princeville, NC, July 30, 2012 and LGC came into Princeville town hall on July 31, 2012 with an authority force requesting files. I saw town files left all over board room and conference room by LGC staff even after working hours left unattended. Then at the end of each day, the LGC staff would take the town original files with them back to Raleigh without documentation and without approval by former interim town manager Maggie Boyd. I would show the LGC staff where files were and they then would take what they wanted. I never saw them return the original files while I was working at Princeville town Hall.

I also witnessed receipts from former interim town manager, Maggie Boyd, from a LGC business meeting trip on July 10, 2013, given to former financial officer, Dianne Draughn, town clerk, and later can't be found. It became very difficult finding files that were needed to complete work.

This 7th day of January, 2014

Daisy L. Staton

Daisy E. Staton

Subscribed and sworn before me this ___7th___ day of January, 2014

Michele Sylvester

Notary Public

My commission expires __01/03/2018__

205

17 Felony Charges: NOT GUILTY

Henry McKoy – he worked with me and my administration. He currently serves as the Assistant Secretary for Commerce for the NC Dept of Commerce in Raleigh, NC.

1

2

3

4 I, Henry McKoy, declare as follows:

5   1. This Affidavit and Declaration is submitted voluntarily and of my own free will. I have

6   personal knowledge of all facts set forth below and if called to testify, I could and would

7   testify competently to these facts.

8   2. I am a citizen of Durham, North Carolina. My educational background is as follows: I

9   have an undergraduate degree in Business Administration from the Kenan-Flagler

10   Business School at the University of North Carolina at Chapel Hill; I have a Master's

11   Degree in Environmental Management, Policy, and Leadership from the Nicholas School

12   of the Environment at Duke University; and I am currently a Ph.D. candidate in the

13   Department of City and Regional Planning at the University of North Carolina at Chapel

14   Hill. I served as Assistant Secretary of Community Development at the North Carolina

15   Department of Commerce from August 2010 until August 2012. I was appointed by

16   Former Governor Beverly Perdue. During my tenure I first had contact with Mayor

17   Priscilla Oates in or about November 2010, and actively worked with Mayor Oates

18   through 2011, and into 2012. In addition to my own work with Mayor Oates, I also had a

19   team staff assigned to her projects, including Oliver Bass and Vanessa Blanchard. Oliver

20   Bass led the team of planners on our part and also met with John Morck, the Director of

21   the Planning Division, to advance the areas of development we could assist with for the

22   Town of Princeville.

23   3. I am aware that Oliver Bass had meetings with Mayor Oates and Princeville Planning

24   Board regularly. I encouraged and suggested Mayor Oates to conduct frequent planning

25   meetings in order to be the most competitive for the grant programs offered by the NC

26   Department of Commerce's Division of Community Assistance. I suggested Mayor Oates

    and Princeville Economic Development Committee Team to consider hosting frequent

    meetings in between meeting with our team in order to be fully prepared for our

AFFIDAVIT AND DECLARATION

DECLARATION OF HENRY MCKOY

1

Team. My team and I were genuinely excited about the projects we were working on with the Mayor and Princeville Economic Development Committee Team.

6. I am aware that Mayor Oates had great interest in reaching out to the citizens of Princeville to bring forth their ideas for small business development. I am also aware that she and Princeville Economic Development Committee Team were working on identifying and applying for appropriate grants to pay for some of the envisioned programs.

7. The Water and Sewer project was presented as a priority to me, therefore it was a primary focus of my team's work with Princeville. According to Mayor Oates and her team, the water and sewer project was assessed at a cost of approximately $7 million. We were looking at total project plans for Princeville estimated at $50 million. We were discussing support of approximately $2-3 million in grants to the Town of Princeville. The planning was halted by the accusations against Mayor Oates. I was very disappointed that the work with Princeville could not go forward.

8. Since I was aware that Mayor Oates and the Princeville Economic Development Committee Team was working so diligently with all of Princeville's projects, I personally visited Princeville and met with Mayor Oates on at least three (3) occasions: a tour of Princeville, the Summit, and the Town Birthday celebration. In addition, I frequently spoke to Mayor Oates by phone and received reports from Oliver Bass regarding progress. (Exhibit 1- Support Letter) and (Exhibit 2 – the Survival Week Program).

9. As to the charges in the indictment against Mayor Oates, I was aware that Mayor Oates, the Princeville Economic Development Committee Team, Reginald Smith and Wallace Green met on many occasions throughout 2010, 2011 and 2012 specifically to work on aspects of the proposed economic development projects for Princeville. To my knowledge, Mayor Oates and Princeville Economic Development Committee Team held these meetings in Raleigh, Durham and Rocky Mount. From my professional and personal experience, I am aware of the need for gasoline expenses, and of the reasonable expectation of needing to pay for meals associated with these meetings.

DECLARATION OF HENRY MCKOY

10. In my experience, Mayor Oates has never conducted herself other than in a professional and correct manner in her dealings with me. She strikes me as a person who wants to genuinely help her town and has, to my knowledge, shown no inclination to enrich herself in any way at the expense of Princeville residents.

//
//
//
//
//
//
//
//

I declare under penalty of perjury under the laws of the State of North Carolina that the foregoing is true, and that this declaration was executed on June 9, 2014, at Durham, North Carolina.

HENRY MCKOY

DECLARATION OF HENRY MCKOY

208

Priscilla E. Oates

PO Box 12442

Research Triangle Park, NC 27709

Monday, September 30, 2013

In 2011, while serving as Assistant Secretary of Community Development at the North Carolina Department of Commerce, I assigned a cross-divisional team from within the Community Development Division to work closely with the City of Princeville and Mayor Priscilla Oates to help with economic and community development planning in the Princeville community. Representatives from the Community Investment and Assistance Division, Rural Development Division, and Community Planning Division were assigned to work.

The task of this workgroup was to work with leadership from Princeville, including Mayor Priscilla Oates and her representatives on strategies that would lead to more sustainable economic development in Princeville. It is the mission of the Community Development Division of NC Commerce to work with cities and towns all across the state to help them prosper. The Community Development Division has a specific focus on working with towns classified as "non-entitlement," which are those communities with populations of under 50,000. Princeville is a non-entitlement community. The Division was also established by North Carolina statute to focus its attention on assisting low-income geographies across the state, of which Princeville is one.

The project team from NC Commerce was to work closely with the Town of Princeville on a full slate of economic directives including capacity building, infrastructure, small business development, affordable quality housing and community planning assistance. The goal was to work with Princeville leadership in a comprehensive way to drive local economic growth. The engagement between Princeville and the NC Department of Commerce had no set time limit, but instead was open. This engagement included site visits by Commerce officials to potential projects in Princeville, as well as meetings in Raleigh at Community Development Central Office.

Though Princeville faced many challenges, we always found Mayor Priscilla Oates and her team to be committed to the goal of creating a stronger and more prosperous community.

Sincerely,

Henry C. McKoy, Jr.

NC Assistant Secretary of Commerce

2010-2012

17 Felony Charges: NOT GUILTY

PRINCEVILLE SURVIVOR WEEK CELEBRATION

PRINCEVILLE TOWN RESOURCES TRAINING SUMMIT

Morning Empowerment Speaker

Mr. Henry McKoy
Assistant Secretary for Commerce

North Carolina Department of Commerce

Raleigh, North Carolina

Friday, November 18, 2011 * 8:45 a.m.

Linking the Local, State, and National (Federal) Thomas S. Fleming Building, Mobley Atrium Edgecombe Community College, Tarboro Campus 2009 West Wilson Street, Tarboro, North Carolina 27886

G.K. Butterfield – member of U.S. Congress who was a great supporter of my administration. Atty Bonner sent him an email regarding him testifying at my trial:

Dear Attorney Roumel,

Thank you very much for you time and studious attention during our telephone conversation regarding Congressman Butterfield testifying in the trial of Mayor Priscilla Everette-Oates.

Attached is the letter from Congressman Butterfield to Mayor Oates. Also attached is the 17 count Indictment involving approximately $5.000 over a 2 1/2 year period relating to expenses such as meal, hotels, gas incurred for the Town of Princeville's Economic Development Committee.

Some of the Charges also involved the expenses during the time Mayor Oates traveled to meet with the Congressman.

As mentioned, the trial is presently set for September 8, 2014 in the Superior Court of Edgecombe County, in the City of Tarboro N.C.

We would like serve a subpoena on the Congressman through you for his appearance during the week of September 15.

As you informed me, Congress is in session during this time so we will give you sufficient advance notice of the date and time we will need the congressman to testify.

We would like to have a pre-testimony conference call with you and the Congressman to discuss the areas of his testimony.

We will call the Congressman as our first witness (to be followed by Durham N.C. Mayor William Bell) and we should be able to get him on and off the stand in about 30 minute.

Also, as discussed, Mr. Russ Haddad's testimony is very much needed as he met with Mayor Oates to help with the Town of Princeville's Economic Development Committee as a referral from Congressman Butterfield.

Again, thank you, and please reach me on my cell: (415).601-0268.

Charles

Charles A. Bonner
Law Offices of Bonner & Bonner
475 Gate Five Rd, Suite 212
Sausalito, CA 94965
tel 415-331-3070
fax 415-331-2738
email: charles@bonnerlaw.com

Priscilla E. Oates

CONGRESS OF THE UNITED STATES
HOUSE OF REPRESENTATIVES

September 12, 2013

The Honorable Priscilla Everette-Oates
Mayor
Town of Princeville
P.O. Box 1527
Princeville, North Carolina 27886

Dear Mayor Everette-Oates:

This letter is in response to your request for information regarding Mr. Russ Haddad's outreach to the Town of Princeville's Economic Development Committee.

Mr. Haddad served as Director of Economic Development and Business Outreach from 2010 – 2012 in my Wilson district office. As part of his role, Mr. Haddad was responsible for assisting municipalities in the First Congressional District of North Carolina with identifying federal resources available to qualifying local governments.

He provided information regarding federal funding opportunities to the Town of Princeville, which is located in the First Congressional District, to further the goal of economic development in eastern North Carolina.

Thank you very much.

Very truly yours,

G. K. Butterfield
Member of Congress

——————— BUTTERFIELD.HOUSE.GOV ———————

WASHINGTON, DC
RAYBURN HOB
WASHINGTON, DC 20515
W: (202) 225-3101
(202) 225-3354

DURHAM
411 WEST CHAPEL HILL STREET
SUITE 905
DURHAM, NC 27701
PHONE: (919) 908-0164
FAX: (919) 908-0167

WILSON
216 NE NASH STREET
SUITE B
WILSON, NC 27893
PHONE: (252) 237-9816
FAX: (252) 291-0356

WELDON
309 WEST THIRD STREET
WELDON, NC 27890
PHONE: (252) 338-4123

941-A

213

17 Felony Charges: NOT GUILTY

Wallace Green – resident of Raleigh, NC and president of Raleigh Area Development Authority (RADA)

AFFIDAVIT AND DECLARATION OF WALLACE GREEN

I, Wallace Green, declare as follows:

1. This Confirmation and Declaration is submitted voluntarily and of my own free will. I have personal knowledge of all facts set forth below and if called to testify, I could and would testify competently to these facts.

2. My educational background is as follows: In 1970, I obtained my Bachelor Degree in the field of Political Science from Morgan Statue University. In 1971 I received my Master's Degree in Communications from Boston University. And I am a licensed real estate broker in the state of North Carolina.

3. I am a resident of Raleigh, North Carolina. I am the President of the Raleigh Area Development Authority (RADA). RADA is a non-profit company whose purpose, goals, and mission are improving quality of life for low income persons through effective economic development programs and services. My duties and responsibilities include all aspects of financial, administrative, and program management. The following are some of the projects RADA has accomplished in the past 10 years under my leadership: 1) established small business loan program; 2) rehabilitated several affordable homes for sale to lower income families; 3) assisted hundreds of NC homeowners in saving their homes from foreclosure.

4. I met Mayor Oates as a result of my organization's interest in being of help to an historic town that might benefit from our experience in economic development strategies.

5. This statement is to confirm that I and other representatives of the Raleigh Area Development Authority (RADA) participated in multiple meetings with Mayor Oates and

various staff members of the Town of Princeville regarding economic development strategies and projects.

6. These meetings, and others in which other people participated, resulted in the development of the attached document which summarized the various roads to meaningful and profitable economic development for the impoverished Town of Princeville. We discussed and strategized regarding opportunities which were determined to have the potential for job creation, the Princeville Economic Development Committee's vision for the Town, Princeville strategic initiatives, Princeville historic and current conditions, 21st century mission planning, Princeville community assessment, development of a Princeville shopping center, a grocery store, and technologies for the production of electricity. These discussions included the Town growth, Implementation Plans for the Town of Princeville, Princeville short term initiative plans, plans for the Princeville Museum and Welcome Center, attraction of private investment, plans for Princeville Tourism and Historical Preservation and updates on progress reports, as well as the promotion of tourism to the area.

7. The vision for the Town also included a very exciting plan for a Biomass Digester for energy production which could have generated an income of approximately $200,000 per year for Princeville. We also planned for a small theme park, focused on reenactments of the slave trade and the establishment of the town. Princeville sits on an extremely rich aquifer of water, and our discussions included the utilization of this aquifer.

8. All of these meetings I attended were narrowly focused on a vision and the realization of this vision for the Town of Princeville. Mayor Oates was always focused on business. I and other members of my company were very excited about the projects we envisioned for

2

17 Felony Charges: NOT GUILTY

Princeville, particularly because Princeville was essentially like a laboratory, it needed everything. I was extremely disappointed that the projects did not go forward. Mayor Oates worked extremely hard on the plans.

9. The Development Plan I created originated from these many and regular meetings, and at no time did I see a motive of self-enrichment in Mayor Oates' actions. She was a meticulous and tireless planner, and when talking about her vision for the Town and the citizens of Princeville, she would say, "Just trying to get to Heaven". (EXHIBIT _19_, Development Plan)

10. Persons representing the Town in these 2010 and 2011 meetings, which were scheduled by the former Town Manager Victor Marrow, were held in Raleigh, Rocky Mount, and Princeville, included Mayor Oates, Mayor Pro Tempore Andrews, Town Manager Victor Marrow, and Reginald Smith. (EXHIBIT _19_, letter dated September 16, 2013).

11. Based on my personal knowledge, I know that Mayor Oates and the Economic Development Committee team incurred ordinary, necessary and customary expenses such as gas, meals and incidentals while traveling from Princeville to Raleigh and back; from Rocky Mount to Princeville and back to meet with me and other representatives of the Raleigh Area Development Authority (RADA) for economic development and progress of the Town of Princeville.

12. Regarding Count I: On August 6, 2010, I attended a meeting in Raleigh with Mayor Oates, Mayor Pro Tem Andrews, Town Manager Victor Marrow, and Reginald Smith for an economic development planning session. The discussion regarding brainstorming on the Princeville's visions and initiative strategies. Therefore, to my personal knowledge, there incurred food and fuel charges.

13. On August 25, 2010, I attended a meeting at the Madison Steak and Seafood Restaurant in Rocky Mount with Mayor Oates, Mayor Pro Tem Andrews, Town Manager Victor Marrow, and Reginald Smith for an economic development planning session. The discussion regarded planning of Princeville's visions and initiative strategy plans. Mayor Oates and Princeville Economic Development Committee drove to the meeting. Therefore, to my personal knowledge, there incurred food and fuel charges.

14. I have reviewed all the allegations in Count I of the indictment and can and do hereby attest that all of these expenses were used for the benefit of the Town of Princeville.

15. Regarding Count II: On September 10, 2010, I attended a meeting in Raleigh with Mayor Oates, Mayor Pro Tem Andrews, Town Manager Victor Marrow, and Reginald Smith for an economic development planning session meeting. The discussion centered on Princeville historic and current conditions. Therefore, to my personal knowledge, there incurred food and fuel charges.

16. On September 21, 2010, I attended a meeting at the Madison Steak and Seafood Restaurant in Rocky Mount with Mayor Oates, Mayor Pro Tem Andrews, Town Manager Victor Marrow, and Reginald Smith for an economic development planning session.

17. I have reviewed all the allegations in Count II of the indictment and can and do hereby attest that all of these expenses were used for the benefit of the Town of Princeville.

18. Regarding Count III: On October 5, 2010, I attended a meeting at the Madison Steak and Seafood Restaurant in Rocky Mount with Mayor Oates, Mayor Pro Tem Andrews, Town Manager Victor Marrow, and Reginald Smith for an economic development planning session. The discussion centered on Princeville community assessment. Mayor Oates and

17 Felony Charges: NOT GUILTY

Princeville Economic Development Committee drove to the meeting in Rocky Mount. Therefore, to my personal knowledge, there incurred food and fuel charges.

19. On October 21, 2010, I attended a meeting in Raleigh with Mayor Oates, Mayor Pro Tem Andrews, Town Manager Victor Marrow, and Reginald Smith, to discuss the Princeville problems and opportunities for the Town's growth. Therefore, to my personal knowledge, there incurred food and fuel charges.

20. I have reviewed all the allegations in Count III of the indictment and can and do hereby attest that all of these expenses were used for the benefit of the Town of Princeville.

21. Regarding Count IV: On November 5, 2010, I attended a meeting in Raleigh with Mayor Oates, Town Manager Victor Marrow, and Reginald Smith for an economic development planning session. The discussion regarded development of a Princeville shopping center, grocery store, and technologies for the production of electricity. Therefore, to my personal knowledge, there incurred food and fuel charges.

22. I have reviewed all the allegations in Count IV of the indictment and can and do hereby attest that all of these expenses were used for the benefit of the Town of Princeville.

23. Regarding Count V: On December 3, 2010, I attended a meeting in Raleigh with Mayor Oates, Mayor Pro Tem Andrews, Town Manager Victor Marrow, and Reginald Smith for an economic development planning session. The discussion centered on our continued discussions and on Implementation plans and community plans for Princeville. Therefore, to my personal knowledge, there incurred food and fuel charges.

24. I have reviewed all the allegations in Count V of the indictment and can and do hereby attest that all of these expenses were used for the benefit of the Town of Princeville.

Priscilla E. Oates

25. Regarding Count VI: On January 13, 2011, I attended a meeting in Raleigh with Mayor Oates, Mayor Pro Tem Andrews, Town Manager Victor Marrow, and Reginald Smith for an economic development planning session. The discussion regarding Princeville short term initiative planning meeting. Therefore, to my personal knowledge, there incurred food and fuel charges.

26. I have reviewed all the allegations in Count VI of the indictment and can and do hereby attest that all of these expenses were used for the benefit of the Town of Princeville.

27. Regarding Count IX: On April 1, 2011, I attended a meeting in Raleigh with Mayor Oates, Mayor Pro Tem Andrews, Town Manager Victor Marrow, and Reginald Smith for and economic development planning session. The discussion regarding Tourism, Princeville museum, and welcome center. Therefore, to my personal knowledge, there incurred food and fuel charges.

28. I have reviewed all the allegations in Count IX of the indictment and can and do hereby attest that all of these expenses were used for the benefit of the Town of Princeville.

29. Regarding Count XI: On June 10, 2011, I attended a meeting at the Madison Steak and Seafood Restaurant in Rocky Mount with Mayor Oates, Mayor Pro Tem Andrews, and Town Manager Victor Marrow for an economic development planning session. The discussion was to continue to discuss and plan on the Implementation plans, Infrastructure designs, and projects. Therefore, to my personal knowledge, there incurred food and fuel charges.

30. I have reviewed all the allegations in Count XI of the indictment and can and do hereby attest that all of these expenses were used for the benefit of the Town of Princeville.

17 Felony Charges: NOT GUILTY

31. Regarding Count XII: On July 8, 2011, I attended a meeting at the Madison Steak and Seafood Restaurant in Rocky Mount with Mayor Oates, Mayor Pro Tem Andrews, Town Manager Victor Marrow, and Reginald Smith for an economic development planning session. The discussion centered on Princeville Tourism and Historical Preservation, and on Progress report updates. Therefore, to my personal knowledge, there incurred food and fuel charges.

32. On July 15, 2011, I attended a meeting at the Madison Steak and Seafood Restaurant in Rocky Mount with Mayor Oates, Mayor Pro Tem Andrews, Town Manager Victor Marrow, and Reginald Smith for an economic development planning session. The discussion and follow up were regarding fast food restaurants, a grocery store, research funds for projects for the Town of Princeville. Mayor Oates and Princeville Economic Development Committee drove to the meeting in Rocky Mount. Therefore, to my personal knowledge, there incurred food and fuel charges.

33. On July 22, 2011, I attended a meeting at the Madison Steak and Seafood Restaurant in Rocky Mount with Mayor Oates, Mayor Pro Tem Andrews, Town Manager Victor Marrow, and Reginald Smith for an economic development planning session. The discussion continued regarding development of a Princeville shopping center, grocery store, and technologies for the production of electricity. Mayor Oates and Princeville Economic Development Committee drove to the meeting. Therefore, to my personal knowledge, there incurred food and fuel charges.

34. I have reviewed all the allegations in Count XII of the indictment and can and do hereby attest that all of these expenses were used for the benefit of the Town of Princeville.

Priscilla E. Oates

35. As I have stated, I have reviewed all the allegations in all counts of the indictment and can and do hereby attest that all of these expenses were used for the benefit of the Town of Princeville.

36. I met Mr. Reginald Smith, the consultant several times at discussion meetings with the Princeville Economic Development Committee. I found him to be knowledgeable about economic development for cities and municipalities.

37. On November 17 - 18, 2011, I attended Princeville Survival Seminar week conference held at Edgecombe Community College in Tarboro with Mayor Oates, Mayor Pro-Tem Andrews, Town Manager Victor Marrow, many distinguished speakers, community leaders, guests, and people from the surrounding area, out of Town, and out of State. I was one of the guests who did a workshop during that time. (Exhibit _37_).

I declare under penalty of perjury under the laws of the State of North Carolina that the foregoing is true, and that this declaration was executed on June___30___, 2014, at _____Raleigh_____, North Carolina.

WALLACE GREEN

17 Felony Charges: NOT GUILTY

PRINCEVILLE ECONOMIC DEVELOPMENT PROJECTS

TO: Mayor Priscilla Everett-Oates
               Victor Marrow
FROM: Wallace Green (919.630.0180)

DATE: June 29, 2011

PROJECT	Objectives and Status
306 Mutual Boulevard Deed Book 1151 Page 250	• Property has been listed for sale with Coldwell Banker Commercial TradeMark Properties (Wallace Green) • Objective is sale to a retail business, including fast food, grocery, or a financial institution. • A small grocery store chain may be interested in the site if a 10,000 sq.ft. building can be constructed. Discussion is needed asap re sources of funding for site work and building construction. (see below re 308 Mutual)
308 Mutual Boulevard	• Acquistion of 308 Mutual is critical to attracting a retail business. Together with 306 Mutual, the properties will total 1.56 acres, approximately the same size as the Dollar General property, which is 1.33 acres. • The house on the property must be relocated • The Town is working on this.
Relocation of Fire Department	• Town is working on this.

Princeville Business Park	• Coldwell Banker TMP is focused on contacting all property owners along Ridgewood Road, from Commercial Road to State Highway 33 to participate in a marketing program to attract new investment and jobs to Princeville.
	• The Town should place contact all property owners in this area inviting to allow the Town to designate the area as Princeville Business Park. The Town should pay for 2 large signs on the property "Princeville Business Park" and the Coldwell Banker TMP phone number. The signs should be visible from Hwy 64. CB can assist with the design.
	• Properties now listed for Sale by CB:
	    1. The former truck stop
	    2.
	    3.

Princeville BioEnergy Project	• Secure a commitment from the Edgecombe- Martin County EMC to purchase renewable energy from a bio-energy system that would be designed and constructed for the Town • The Town Manager is arranging a preliminary meeting to be attended by Wallace Green who has identified a technology provider to design and construct the system. • The Town will need to raise the necessary funds for construction and operation of the system. The budget will depend upon the agreement with the EMC.
Feasibility of Town owned Waste and Drinking Water Treatment utility	• A private equity fund has expressed interest in conducting a feasibility study. Information regarding the fund is located at the following web site, and the Mayor is advised to consult with the Town attorney about how best to proceed with an initial discussion about the potential approach. www.AmericanInfrastructureInvestors.com NOTE: The result of this type of transaction would mean that the system is designed, built, and operated by the investor. Financial benefits to the Town would be negotiated, thus the need to discuss this with the Town attorney.
Grant Writing	The following grants are being prepared at your request: | Grantor&Writer	Purpose/Status	Due Date
---	---	---
EPA	Brownfields Assessment re Ridgewood site, and Mutual Blvd. site; Waiting on call from Atlanta office	TBD

223

17 Felony Charges: NOT GUILTY

From: wgreen@cbctmp.com
To: mayoroates@townofprinceville.org, vam02@aol.com
Cc: wallace.green@rada-nc.com, wgreen@cbctmp.com
Subject: Follow Up Discussion Topics

Date: Wed, 1 Jun 2011 02:21:23 -0400

Discussion Topics re Princeville Economic Development

1. **Marketing Retail Site on Mutual Boulevard** -- now that we have a listing I have asked the Coldwell Banker team to begin identifying prospects for a fast food restaurant franchise. I will also contact the state-wide credit union organization to determine if there is interest in the location or the current fire department location. I need to know what liens there are on the property we just listed, and by whom. ALSO, IT IS CRITICAL THAT WE GET THE SITE NEXT TO IT UNDER CONTRACT SINCE THE FIRST TRACT IS NOT LARGE ENOUGH.

2. **Relocation of Fire Department** -- the current fire department site will make a good retail location and we may be able to access Building Reuse funds from the State to prepare it for a new tenant once we have a prospect.

3. **Renewable Energy Project** -- Mayor will contact the Electrical Cooperative to discuss a Power Purchase Agreement (PPA) that will help us secure financing to build a facility that would be owned by the Town that will produce electricity.

4. **Water Treatment Plant** -- I have called a Raleigh engineering company Stephanie Norris (919.669.1079) to learn more about what process is required for Princeville to own and operate its own water utility; this could also help create a new business that would produce high quality water for the pharmaceutical industry. Potential sites would then be investigated with the help of an engineer.

5. **Princeville Business Park** -- I met this week with my Coldwell Banker team about making contact with all owners of properties along Ridgewood from Commercial Drive to Route 33. This is more than 30 acres including the old truck stop. We need to discuss a small amount of funding for putting up signs for "Princeville Business Park" and also about State and County incentives that will help us to attract businesses to purchase sites. This area is also the site targeted for the Renewable Energy Project, and maybe the pharmaceutical water company.

6. **Relocation of the house on Mutual Boulevard** for use by the Police Department. What is status of this?

Wallace O. Green
Commercial Real Estate Broker
Director, Public Private Partnerships
919.630.0180

Priscilla E. Oates

AFFIDAVIT

I, Mayor Pro Tem Andrews do hereby swear and affirm that Reggie Smith was a Consultant with the Town of Princeville Economic Development. He got paid by the Former Manager/Budget Officer, Victor Marrow, doing the same time payroll. I was one of the Town designated signee on the Town checks. I signed the majority of Reggie Smith's checks after the Former Manager/Budget Officer signed or initialed the invoices. I also contact the current Interim Town Clerk to get me a copy of Reggie Smith's contract. She stated that she didn't see any files on Reggie Smith. As I have stated to Agent Lolita Chapman on June 11, 2013, that all of Princeville's files has gone missing since LGC took over the Town's books and finances.

This the 21th day of June, 2013

Isabelle Purvis-Andrews

Isabelle Purvis-Andrews, Mayor Pro Tem

Subscribed and sworn before me this the __21st__ day of June, 2013.

Catherine Hinton

Notary Public

My commission expires __11/18/17__

2   DA000695

17 Felony Charges: NOT GUILTY

AFFIDAVIT

I, Mayor Pro Tem Andrews do hereby swear and affirm that I was part of the Princeville Economic Development Committee. I did attend the majority of those meetings. I have seen Mayor Oates paid and put receipts in a zip lock bag. I have seen Mayor Oates turned her receipts and documents in the majority of the time to the Former Town Clerk/Finance Officer. I was one of the designated signee on the Town checks. I only signed the checks after the Former Town Manager/Budget Officer Victor Marrow signed or initialed the invoices with the receipts and supported documents attached.

The Mayor and I have learned in our first term that we need to be a witness for one another.

This the 24th day of June, 2013

Isabelle Purvis-Andrews

Isabelle Purvis-Andrews, Mayor Pro Tem

Subscribed and sworn before me this the 24th day of June, 2013

Catherine Hinton

Notary Public

My commission expires 11/18/17

3   DA000696

11.
Tonya Montanye

This was the lead prosecutor on my case and she also used Sharon Edmundson's spreadsheet to create the charges to indict me. Montanye testified that her intention was not to look for missing receipts but to confirm that purchases made did not have a true business purpose. She used the Economic Development Committee to justify that to her knowledge, no such committee existed.

Montanye discussed the indictment she was proposing with SBI Agent Chapman and it is my understanding that that Chapman agreed with Montanye that the committee did not exist. They went through with the charges and I was indicted on all 17 counts on August 7, 2013.

After I was arrested, LGC still had all of the books and financial documents at their office. Holloman and the LGC team were given subpoenas to request all the records be given back and they refused, only to make their own request to quash (reject or put an end to something) the subpoenas.

Thank goodness the court denied their motion and in September 2014, the court ordered prosecution and my defense attorneys to be allowed to do an on-site inspection of the records at the LGC office.

After a two-day inspection, we successfully found the hidden documents! Thank God for Judge Osmond Smith's

Order. There was a storage closet filled with pretty much all the financial records for Princeville in addition to more records that Edmundson had in her office. The documents contained all the proof and back-up to confirm I had not done anything wrong or illegal. There were handwritten notes included on all the receipts I had submitted with purchases. Again, everything had been hidden and concealed inside the LGC office!

The following pages include a portion of her deposition and the dismissal email Montanye emailed to D.A. Robert Evans, and the Indictment Dismissal Order filed with the court, which reinstated my business and confirmed charges would be dropped!

You may scan the QR code to read Montanye's deposition in its entirety:

SCAN HERE

Priscilla E. Oates

EMAIL

Re: State of NC v. Priscilla Everette-Oates, Edgecombe County File Number 13 CRS 2056

Tonya Oliver Montanye - Eastern NC Financial Crimes Prosecutor March 19, 2015

The Honorable Robert A. Evans
District Attorney
Prosecutorial District 7

Rocky Mount Judicial Center
PO Box 232
Rocky Mount, NC 27802

Re: State of NC v. Priscilla Everette-Oates, Edgecombe County File Number 13 CRS 2056

Dear Mr. Evans,

I am writing to you concerning the above-referenced matter where the defendant, the former mayor of the Town of Princeville, was charged with seventeen felony counts of embezzlement by a public official. As you are aware, this matter was investigated by Agent L. Chapman of the North Carolina State Bureau of Investigation (SBI) after concerns regarding possible criminal conduct concerning the use of the Town's credit card by the then current mayor of Princeville were brought to the attention of you and the SBI by the Local Government Commission (LGC), a division of the Secretary of Treasury's Office, and the Office of the State Auditor (OSA). In fact, OSA issued a report concerning its investigation of the Princeville mayor's credit card expenditures. The OSA report was provided to you and later to me; the report was also made public. The OSA file, however, was not provided to the District Attorney's Office or to the Conference of District Attorneys' Financial Crimes Unit. (In fact, in August 2014, OSA contested and successfully defended a request by the defense for these documents as a general statute provides that their file will remain confidential.)

While much of the focus of the OSA's report was the lack of receipts provided by Mayor Everette-Oates for her credit card charges, the criminal investigation did not rely solely on the lack of receipts. Instead, the criminal investigation focused on credit card charges for meals and gas that did not appear to be legitimate business expenditures.

In making the charging decision, much attention was given to those charges that were reportedly for the Economic Development Committee. Before making a charging decision, I personally, along with SBI Agent Chapman, was advised that no such committee existed. I was advised of this by LGC employees Vance Holloman and Sharon Edmundson.

You may scan the QR code to read in its entirety:

17 Felony Charges: NOT GUILTY

The fact that the committee did not exist was reiterated to me on numerous occasions both in person and over the telephone before a charging decision was made and throughout the prosecution of this matter. I was also advised repeatedly by those same individuals that the mayor did not provide receipts. After these discussions, a thorough review of the SBI report provided by Agent Chapman, and careful consideration, the decision was made to indict Mayor Everette-Oates for seventeen felony counts of embezzlement by a public official. The Grand Jury of Edgecombe County returned a true bill for those charges on August 5, 2013.

After indictment, discovery was provided to Mayor Everette-Oates original attorney, Joseph Hester. A written plea offer was also extended to Mr. Hester in December 2013 allowing the defendant to plead to three counts, pay $5,633.94 restitution and dismiss the remaining charges. That offer was rejected. In the spring of 2014, Defendant retained new counsel, Charles Bonner, an attorney from California appeared pro hac vice, having associated himself with Ryan Stump and Samuel Randall, attorneys from Charlotte, NC. This matter was then set for trial in September of 2014.

In preparation for trial, I began personally interviewing witnesses. I interviewed the former Town Manager, Victor Marrow, who confirmed in his interview that the mayor routinely did not provide receipts. I also interviewed the former Town Clerk, Diana Draughn, who likewise confirmed that the Mayor usually did not provide receipts. During my trial preparation, I also interviewed Andrew Harris who had performed financial work for the Town. Mr. Harris had not previously been interviewed by the SBI. He, likewise, confirmed that lack of supporting documentation for credit card expenditures was a huge issue that he had while working on the financials for the Town. All three witnesses advised that they were not aware of an Economic Development Committee. SBI Agent Chapman was present during all three interviews. I also met with and interviewed former Princeville mayor Delia Perkins. Like Mr. Harris, Ms. Perkins had not been interviewed previously by the SBI. Ms. Perkins advised that she was the mayor who directly preceded Mayor Everette Oates. Ms. Perkins advised that she had an Economic Development Committee but never took trips out of the town of Princeville for meetings. She advised that it was not a formal committee in the sense that the Town Council had created the committee but was an executive committee and that the mayor is allowed to have executive committees. Again, Agent Chapman was present for this interview in which Ms. Perkins shared this information.

I also met with Robin Hammond, Vance Holloman, and Sharon Edmundson to prepare for trial in August of 2014. Agent Chapman was also present. During this meeting which was held in the LGC conference room on the second floor, Sharon Edmundson advised that I should make contact with Phyllis Pearson, a certified public accountant from Zebulon, who had performed the town audit which essentially triggered this investigation as it contained negative or adverse findings.

Ms. Pearson had never been interviewed by the SBI. Ms. Edmundson also advised me that they were not aware of who had created a spreadsheet that had been used during the investigation of this matter. While preparing for trial, I emailed Sharon Edmundson requesting all receipts belonging to the mayor that LGC had in their possession. I received an email on August 7, 2014, with what appears to be seventeen receipts attached. The email only included the front of those receipts. Many times while requesting information from LGC, I was advised, particularly by Ms. Edmundson, that almost the information that they had pertaining to Princeville had been returned to the Town. I also was often advised that the reason that they were not able to provide this information was because Mayor Everette-Oates had not turned the documentation in as she should. After being provided the name of Phyllis Pearson, Ms. Pearson was interviewed by myself, Financial Crimes Prosecutor W. Scott Harkey of the Piedmont region, and Agent Chapman at Ms. Pearson's office. Ms. Pearson again reiterated that many receipts for the mayor's expenditures had not been provided to her while conducting the town audit. After being provided with a subpoena, Ms. Pearson produced her workpapers pertaining to the town audit. Upon reviewing her work papers and her report, it was discovered that former town manager Victor Marrow was mentioned in the audit for his own excessive use of the Town's gas credit card.

Likewise, former Town Clerk Diana Draughn was also discussed in the report concerning her personal vehicle being repaired at the Town's expense (Note that I was aware of this early on, but Ms. Draughn was charged before my assistance was requested, and a plea, wherein the charges would be dismissed, was negotiated by another prosecutor.).

Furthermore, Ms. Pearson's findings placed considerable blame for the mayor's credit card expenditures on the Town Manager, Victor Marrow, for providing the card to the mayor and failing to adequately supervise her expenditures as a town manager should.

As the trial date neared, the defense began requesting information from the LGC. I was repeatedly advised in person, over the phone and by email that the information either did not exist or was not in the possession of the LGC. As I had previously and repeatedly been advised by LGC that the Mayor did not provide documentation of her expenditures, I felt confident that the information was not available. As we got closer and closer to the trial date, the email exchanges between defense counsel and LGC in-house counsel Robin Hammond became uglier and uglier. Shortly before trial, a motion to quash a subpoena issued by defense counsel for information in the possession of the LGC was heard. Bob Curran

from the Attorney General's Office represented the State at the hearing. I was present for the hearing. During the hearing Bob Curran advised the Court, with the Honorable J. Carlton Cole presiding, that the LGC had previously provided a considerable amount of the requested information pursuant to the defense's public records request. The defense quickly pointed out that the LGC had never responded to the public records requests. Accordingly, Judge Cole denied the LGC's motion to quash and ordered the LGC to comply with the subpoena. After this hearing, the email exchanges became even nastier between defense counsel and Ms. Hammond. The LGC did not comply with the subpoena.

17 Felony Charges: NOT GUILTY

On the day trial was to begin, September 8, 2014, members from LGC showed up with partial documentation and advised that it would take them weeks to comply with the request. As a result of LGC's failure to produce, a conference was held in chambers with Judge Osmond Smith. Defense counsel, Ryan Stump and Samuel Randall, co-prosecutor Scott Harkey and I were present. As a result of the conference, the judge continued the matter to October with the understanding that defense counsel and I would go to LGC that week and review all information the LGC had in its possession pertaining to Princeville. The next day, Ryan Stump, Scott Harkey and myself went to the LGC offices in Raleigh, NC, where we were taken into a small room that was full of numerous banker boxes. We were shown all of the boxes that pertained to Princeville and were told that was all that LGC had pertaining to the Town.

Accordingly, all three of us began going through the boxes looking for relevant information.

While there, we found files pertaining to the Mayor's travel including travel request forms and agendas for conferences that the mayor had attended (I had specifically requested this information from the SBI agent during the investigation and was told that it could not be located.). A file labeled "Economic Development Committee" was also located. We were there for three days. On the last day, Sharon Edmundson approached us and told us that she, Robin and Vance all had information in their offices pertaining to Princeville. All of that information was reviewed by us. The last office we went into was Sharon Edmundson's office. Ms. Edmundson advised that she "worked off of those files constantly which is why [she] kept them in her office." In her office, an envelope was found which contained receipts in them. On most, if not all, of the receipts there were handwritten notes pertaining to the purported purpose of the expenditure. The outside of the envelope in which the receipts were found was labeled "appears to be receipts from Diana and the Mayor." These items were sealed and subsequently taken by Agent Chapman. The front and back were copied and provided to the defense. The additional items that were identified as being necessary were left at LGC for them to make copies and provide them to the State and the Defense. Shortly after our visit to LGC, Ryan Stump and I were contacted by Robin Hammond advising us that there was no way LGC would be able to copy the items that we needed so they had taken the liberty of obtaining estimates for an outside agency to copy the items. We were advised that it was approximately 35,000-50,000 pages of items that needed to be copied at an expense of approximately $10,000 which we would have to pay. As a result of this information, Mr. Stump and I had a conference call with Judge Smith where we jointly requested that an order be entered requiring LGC to furnish the documents at their own expense. Judge Smith signed the order, it was served on LGC and they complied with the order furnishing a compact disc to both parties on October 3, 2015.

After the discovery of these items at LGC, I was contacted by members of the LGC on several occasions offering explanations as to the items that were found. In fact, in one telephone conversation with Vance Holloman he downplayed the receipts that were located identifying them instead as "credit card charge slips." I pointed out to Mr. Holloman that the previous receipts that had been provided by LGC when I had requested all receipts pertaining to the mayor were mainly "credit card charge slips" also.

Priscilla E. Oates

Accordingly, classifying the recently located receipts as "credit card charge slips" did not explain LGC's failure to turn over the items when requested by me and the defense. During my telephone conversations with Robin Hammond, Vance Holloman and Sharon Edmundson during the fall of 2014, I explained that there were severe credibility issues and evidentiary issues in the case and that a decision on how to proceed would have to be made. The OSA was advised that additional receipts had been located. The receipts provided were forwarded to Agent Barry Long who investigated this matter for the OSA. An amended report was released by the OSA on December 23, 2014.

On March 12, 2015, Tammy Smith, Financial Crimes Resource Prosecutor with the North Carolina Conference of District Attorneys and my immediate supervisor, and I met with members of LGC in their conference room. Bob Curran, Robin Hammond, Sharon Edmundson, and Greg Gaskins, the new Deputy Treasurer and head of LGC attended on behalf of LGC. Mr. Holloman, the previous Deputy Treasurer and head of LGC during the investigation and prosecution of this matter, had since retired from his position and was now working for the Town of Apex. During the meeting, Ms. Smith and I explained that we had determined that it was in the interest of justice given the problems that now existed in this matter to dismiss the charges against Priscilla Everette-Oates. We explained in general what we anticipated our dismissal and our press release would say. During the meeting, Deputy Treasurer Gaskins repeatedly expressed interest and concern in preventing this from happening in the future.
He advised that an inventory procedure was already in the works to be utilized in the future. Ms. Smith and I both commended them for that new procedure. I reminded everyone that in the future that it would be best to open the LGC office to the investigator early on in the investigation process. While they acknowledged that suggestion, Ms. Hammond did suggest that the SBI agent was to blame. For all the reasons set forth in this letter which I have also expressed to you in person during our meetings on March 4 and March 16, I have recommended that the charges against Priscilla Everette-Oates pertaining to the misuse of the Princeville town credit card be dismissed. Accordingly, I filed a dismissal yesterday and am enclosing a copy for your records. I regret that this matter has turned out as it has but feel that the action taken yesterday is most consistent with our obligation and duty to do justice. If you have any questions, please do not hesitate to contact me at 252-639-3133 or electronically at Tonya.O.Montanye@nccourts.org.

Sincerely,

Tonya Oliver Montanye

Eastern NC Financial Crimes

Prosecutor

Enclosure

Montanye, Tonya O.

Montanye   Direct   -29-

1   mentioned to me then or if it came later.

2   Q   Okay. Is it fair to say that it was fairly early on--

3   A   That--

4   Q   --during your time?

5   A   That's correct.

6   Q   Okay. And if you could--from what you do remember, what

7   all was done to get up to speed on the case?

8   A   I--well, I can't remember very clearly, but it seems that I

9   met with Agent Chapman. And at some point I was

10   provided the SBI report, which included the state auditor's

11   report, and I reviewed that.

12   Q   And when you say the state auditor's report, are you

13   referring to the investigative report?

14   A   I was provided the official report that was released--

15   Q   Okay. And--

16   A   --because I believe that we were invi--we were provided

17   boxes later on towards the end of our case.

18   Q   Okay. And--but you're talking about the report that was

19   put online I believe that--

20   A   Correct.

21   Q   Okay.

22

23

24

Montanye   Direct   -30-

1   A   Correct. And you said you initially met with Agent

2   Q   Chapman and I guess discussed the case. Do you

3   remember he con--the--what consisted--or what you

4   guys talked about during that conversation?

5   A   I don't.

6   Q   Okay.

7   A   And I--I know that I met with Barry Long and another

8   person from the state auditor's office as well, a young

9   man. Bryan maybe is his name. I can't recall--

10   Okay.

11 Q   --without looking at notes or e-mails or something. But I

12 A   don't remember if I met with them at the first meeting--

13 Q   Uh-huh (yes).

14 A   --or if it was later. I just don't remember that.

15 Q   Okay. Do you--and specifically Ms. Chapman--do you recall,

16   while you may not remember the conversation in detail,

17   what she had told you she investigated to that point?

18 A   I--I--I don't really remember any details, I mean. And I will

19   just say from my general practice, you know, I would meet

20   with an--an SBI agent and I

21

22

23

24

17 Felony Charges: NOT GUILTY

1 would, you know, have a brief conversation with them,

2 but I certainly wouldn't make any decisions because I

3 would want to read the report first.

4 Q Okay.

5 A And--and so I know that, you know, that's how I would

6 have handled things.

7 Q Okay. And I guess that's a good point. Is--can you

8 describe as far as--I mean, I believe that you said at this

9 point you had about fifteen years of experience as a

10 prosecutor.

11 A Uh-huh (yes).

12 Q What--for your cases specifically, what was the role of

13 either a detective, SBI agent in the grand scheme of a

14 prosecution or investigation? Well, they're supposed to

15 A conduct the investigation and they're supposed to bring

16 us the report that we can review. And, you know--and

17 oftentimes, you know, we do have conversations with

18 investigators about things. But hopefully everything is--is

19 summarized in the report, you know, or somewhere in the

20 report.

21 Q And specifically as to financial crimes cases, are there

22 certain documents or records that you would expect the

23 agent or detective to review as part of

24

Priscilla E. Oates

1 their investigation?

2 A I mean, well, it depends on what the financial

3 crime is. You know, certainly--

4 Q Let's say it's credit card fraud.

5 A Yes. So I--with a credit card fraud, you know, I would expect

6 them to--I would expect them to have copies of receipts, if

7 there were any. I mean, they've got to show me how it was

8 that the individual that's the suspect used the credit card,

9 so they've got to present evidence of that. You know, do we

10 have the person on video? Does the person admit to using

11 it? Are there witnesses that say the person used it? How is

12 it that we know that it was that individual that used the

13 credit card?

14   You know, in--in this particular case, it would have

15 been the fact that, you know, the credit card was I believe

16 assigned to her. So I--I do remember there were

17 discussions at some point about that. Now, you know, the

18 details of those discussions I don't remember. I do

19 remember, you know, the discussions about the receipts,

20 that she--she told me that a lot of the receipts did-- you

21 know, for the transactions just did not exist.

22

23

24

17 Felony Charges: NOT GUILTY

1   Q   And--I'm sorry--when you say she--

2   A   Sorry. Agent Chapman.

3   Q   Okay.

4   A   I mean, that was one of the things early on, that some of

5   the receipts had been provided and some didn't exist. In

6   this particular case, I know there was a spreadsheet that

7   everybody kind of relied on.

8   Q   Okay.

9   A   And that would have been presented to me early on. But,

10   I mean, again, I think that would have been part of the

11   SBI report.

12   Q   As far as other items you would--or records you would

13   want or assume were reviewed, would you say like credit

14   card statements?

15   A   Yes. Yes. Yes.

16   Q   Okay. What about particularly in this case expense logs?

17   A   Whether or not you're an authorized user and things of

18   that nature. You know, at some point in this case, you

19   know, it was relevant as to what was--you know, was there

20   any kind of policy or procedure in place in regards to

21   credit card use.

22   Q   Okay.

23

24

Pace Reporting Service, Inc.

Wilmington (910) 790-5599   •   Raleigh (919) 859-0000   •   Fayetteville (910) 433-2926

		Montanye	Direct	-34-

1   A   Because, I mean, some places have that--some

2   businesses--some, you know, towns have that; some

3   places don't. You'd be surprised at the number of places

4   that don't have any policy or procedure in place. But

5   that is something that you look for.

6   Q   Okay. What about--

7   A   And whether or not these were approved expenditures too

8   by the--by the board, by the town council.

9   Q   And then what about like expense logs filled out by the

10   employee or the person trying to get reimbursement?

11   A   Right. If that's the way that it had been done. But, I mean,

12   usually I don't think you're getting-- I mean, you know, as a

13   state employee, when I travel, you know, I have to fill out

14   something, and then I get reimbursed. But I don't--you

15   know, it's just a per diem amount. It's a set rate. So I

16   remember asking about that, you know, was there

17   anything in place for that--

18   Q   Okay.

19   A   --and did she fill anything out. But she had a credit

20   card, you know, which is the difference, you know,

21   because, I mean, it appeared that she was just going

22   and, you know, if she needed gas for

23

24

17 Felony Charges: NOT GUILTY

1   driving--because a lot of the transactions were gas use--

2   Q   Okay.

3   A   --and also meals--

4   Q   Okay.

5   A   --if I'm remembering correctly.

6   Q   Would the expense logs be important in evaluating the

7   purpose of the expenditure if that was being filled out per

8   month and submitted with the receipts?

9   A   I think it would be important in the respect that-- you

10   know, first of all, are you supposed to fill them out, you

11   know, again is the policy and procedure and the--or the

12   common practice that you fill them out. And then if that

13   person didn't do so, were they trying to hide something.

14   And then if--once filled out, you know, were they passed

15   on to anybody in authority that then approved it--

16   Q   Okay.

17   A   --you know, whether that be the town manager or the

18   town board. So, I mean, certainly they--they would have

19   been relevant. I--I don't remember being shown any at

20   the beginning, but maybe I was. haven't reviewed any of

21   the stuff coming in to give

22

23

24

1   this deposition--

2 Q Okay.

3 A --so-- So if it was common practice and they were

4 Q submitted as they should be and signed off on, that is

5   something you're saying would be important to be

6   reviewed during the investigation?

7 A I would think so.

8 Q Okay. You stated--I believe you stated also that at some

9   point--I don't know if it was early on--the first conversation

10   or two you had with Agent Chapman, she indicated to you

11   that receipts--the majority of the receipts did not exist. Is

12   that what you stated earlier?

13 A Well--

14   MR. RABINOVITZ: Objection.

15 A --I don't remember how many she said didn't exist,

16   whether she said the majority or--you know, or a lot of

17   them didn't exist. I know that there was discussion--

18   significant discussion throughout the case about the

19   receipts being missing.

20 Q Okay.

21 A And I know at some point it was brought to my

22   attention by people at LGC that the defendant at

23

24

Montanye   Direct   -37-

1   that time, Priscilla Everette-Oates, had filed a police

2   report for missing receipts.

3 Q   Okay.

4 A   That was brought to my attention.

5 Q   As far as Agent Chapman advising you that the receipts--

6   or some portion of the receipts did not exist, did she tell

7   you what she did to ensure that?

8 A   What Agent Chapman always told me was that she was

9   checking with LGC and she was making requests of them.

10 Q   Specifically to the receipts?

11 A   Yes. And, I mean, I--we had numerous discussions about

12   whether or not she ever requested receipts from them.

13 Q   When you say numerous discussions, do you--can you--

14   and--

15   Can I--how many? I don't know. I would say probably--I

16   mean, during the course of the entire investigation, I

17   mean, I would say, you know, five to ten, somewhere in

18 A   there.

19 Q   And--

20 A   I mean, it wasn't discussed just once. And --I mean, and

21   I know that there were times that I

22

23

24

1   requested specific things, such as if you looked at the

2   spreadsheet--because a lot revolved around that

3   spreadsheet--the defendant, Priscilla Everette- Oates, was-

4   -there was numerous occasions where she went to

5   seminars. I mean, I remember one in the Charlotte area

6   and one in--in D.C. And I wanted to know whether or not

7   we had any agendas from there. You know, I said "This is

8   something I want you to look into" because if she was like-

9   -she was clearly getting meals and--and mileage. I mean,

10   well, she was paying for gas--

11   Q   Uh-huh (yes).

12   A   --for those seminars. And so I wanted to know whether

13   or not she had gotten reimbursed through any other

14   means for her mileage. I wanted to know whether or not

15   the meals were being provided as part of the seminar,

16   because for some of mine the meals are provided. And I

17   requested that those--that Agent Chapman get those so

18   that we could look into some further stuff. And she

19   advised that she was unable to locate any.

20   Q   Okay.

21   A   Now, it was my understanding that she had reached out

22   to Local Government Commission requesting that

23

24

1		information and she was advised that that didn't exist. But
2		I was not part of that conversation between Agent
3		Chapman and--
4	Q	And is that--
5	A	--and Local Government Commission.
6	Q	Is that solely related to the agendas of the conferences, or
7		is that the receipts?
8	A	No, to the receipts as well.
9	Q	Okay.
10	A	Yeah. I mean, again, you know, my--my job is to be a
11		prosecutor and to take the evidence that's been given to
12		me and--and to try and prosecute the case. So hopefully,
13		you know, since I have so many cases to focus on the
14		investigator--I can have a conversation with the
15		investigator and say "Request this information"; they make
16		an attem--they attempt to get that information; they
17		advise me whether or not that exists--
18		Okay.
19	Q	--or they were able to get that.
20	A	Okay. And did Agent Chapman ever indicate to you that
21	Q	she had personally reviewed files at the LGC?
22	A	No, she did not.
23	Q	Okay. And I believe you stated that Agent--was it
24		

Priscilla E. Oates

STATE OF NORTH CAROLINA

EDGECOMBE _____ County

FILED

File No.
13CRS2056

In The General Court Of Justice
☐ District   ☒ Superior Court Division

STATE VERSUS

PAR 18 PM 2: 26

Defendant Name

PRISCILLA EVERETTE-OATES

DISMISSAL
NOTICE OF REINSTATEMENT
(For Offenses Committed On Or Before Nov. 30, 2013)

G.S. 15A-302(e), -931, -932, -1009

File Number	Count No.(s)	Offense(s)
13CRS2056	1-17	EMBEZZLEMENT BY A PUBLIC OFFICIAL/TRUSTEE

☒ **DISMISSAL**

NOTE: *Recall all outstanding Orders For Arrest in a dismissed case.*
The undersigned prosecutor enters a dismissal to the above charge(s) and assigns the following reasons:

☐ 1. No crime is charged.

☐ 2. There is insufficient evidence to warrant prosecution for the following reasons:

☐ 3. Defendant has agreed to plead guilty to the following charges:

in exchange for a dismissal of the following charges:

☒ 4. Other: *(specify)*   ☐ See additional information on reverse.

Information discovered subsequent to indictment has come into consideration so that criminal prosecution is not in interest of justice.

A jury has not been impaneled nor has evidence been introduced. *(If a jury has been impaneled, or if evidence has been introduced, modify this sentence accordingly.)*

☐ **DISMISSAL WITH LEAVE**

The undersigned prosecutor enters a dismissal with leave to the above charge(s) and assigns the following reasons:

☐ 1. The defendant failed to appear for a criminal proceeding at which the defendant's attendance was required and the prosecutor believes that the defendant cannot readily be found.

☐ 2. The defendant has been indicted and cannot readily be found to be served with an Order For Arrest.

☐ 3. The defendant has entered into a deferred prosecution agreement with the prosecutor in accordance with the provisions of Article 82 of G.S. Chapter 15A.

☐ 4. The defendant has been found by a court to be incapable of proceeding pursuant to Article 56 of G.S. Chapter 15A.

☐ 5. Other: *(specify)*   ☐ See additional information on reverse.

NOTE: *This form must be completed and signed by the prosecutor when the dismissal occurs out of court. The better practice is for the prosecutor to complete and sign the form when the charges are orally dismissed in open court.*

Also, in accordance with G.S. 15A-931(a1), unless the defendant or the defendant's attorney has been otherwise notified by the prosecutor, a written dismissal of the charges against the defendant must be served in the same manner prescribed for motions under G.S. 15A-951. If the record reflects that the defendant is in custody, the written dismissal shall also be served by the prosecutor on the chief officer of the custodial facility where the defendant is in custody.

Date	Name Of Prosecutor (Type Or Print)	Signature Of Prosecutor
03/18/2015	TONYA OLIVER MONTANYE	

☐ **REINSTATEMENT**

This case, having previously been dismissed with leave as indicated above, is now reinstated for trial.

Date	Name Of Prosecutor (Type Or Print)	Signature Of Prosecutor

AOC-CR-307A, Rev. 12/13   (Over)
© 2013 Administrative Office of the Courts

17 Felony Charges: NOT GUILTY

12.

God gets ALL the glory!

I am a walking testimony that the power of God is real and He is true to what He says. During this entire prosecution, I have experienced everything from pain, anxiety, depression, mental distress, emotional loss and so much more. When all of this was going on, I couldn't believe it. I was amazed. My faith went from fully persuaded into a spiritual coma.

I am often asked how... how did I make it through something like this? How did I survive without losing my mind? I'll tell you: if it had not been for the Lord on my side I would not be here to talk about it and give Him all the glory.

The pain I endured was UNBEARABLE due to shame and my name being scandalized to the world. I experienced so many disappointments and failures in life because of the false allegations during this horrible time. Remember there were 17 *false* allegations that were felonies... charges which would have sent me to prison for 75 years.

The stress and worry caused me to have chest pains, severe headaches, my blood pressure shot up higher than ever; I also had stomach/digestion issues, diarrhea and panic attacks. I suffered so much that I could not focus on my duties for my son and husband.

It took my husband to speak life into me every single day. That's what charged me up but I wasn't dead, though. At night, he would put my earbuds in and turn on Christian music. The Word of God kept charging me up when my faith went into a coma. I couldn't see ahead. My husband kept showing me the vision that we're coming out of this and he was trying to keep me strengthened. He reminded me God still had me... God still had people speaking into me.

If you have never experienced a panic attack, it can be very scary! I was constantly worried, depressed, nervous, uneasy that I was going to spend 75 years in prison for crimes I did not commit! Worrying about that caused me to lose time and my life. My life was lost for the period of time that I had to deal with the lawyers, court proceedings, and dealing with my accusers. I was so busy focusing on my son and husband making sure none of this was affecting them that I didn't sleep at night. Worrying about them added to my stress because I wanted to be sure they knew I was doing everything I could to maintain and prove my innocence.

I frequently experienced panic attacks due to the shock of being falsely accused. Just thinking about it would send me into a panic-driven state almost immediately. I remember while at a restaurant for dinner, I could not eat and had an anxiety attack because the thought - just the thought - of being accused of 17 *felonies* was beyond stressful!

I was very, very worried that if I went to prison for 75 years, my son would have to be raised without a mother, and I didn't want that at all. The bond I had with my son was priceless.

The panic attacks were directly connected to fear. We all know that fear is real and I was fearful of many, many things. I was very fearful of going to prison for 75 years for something I did not do. I was fearful of losing my son and husband. I was very fearful of losing my life through being sick. I was fearful of being in this state of anxiety. I was very fearful of SBI accusing me of something I did not do. I was fearful of losing my son and husband. I was fearful of being in constant anxiety during the investigation. I was definitely fearful of the police coming to my business and destroying it; or them coming to my home and my businesses with a warrant and disrupt the clients, staffs and our neighbors. I couldn't believe it when the SBI placed the yellow tape around my building on scene as if a murder or something had taken place. I was so fearful SBI and police would come to my business and spy on the mental health and substance abuse clients and my home.

As a Christian, a minister, a public servant, a business owner, youth leader, a wife and mother, a family member, and a citizen of United States, I was totally embarrassed and humiliated that my name and reputation was attached to 17 felony crimes that I did not commit. In addition, all of the negative press on the news, in the papers and on social media made me look like I could not be trusted and I was crooked. I had to isolate myself and stay in the house with my husband and my son, and I was not having a good time. There was no recreation, fun times or anything like that.

God Almighty spoke to my heart and said all charges will be dropped and you will stand on My Word. I will deliver you from all of this trouble, and you will truly be a testimony for the NATIONS. God also spoke that my story would be made into a book and a film.

17 Felony Charges: NOT GUILTY

After God spoke all fears left me instantly. It was then that my faith came out of the coma and I regained my faith. I returned to being FULLY PERSUADED.

God **DROPPED ALL 17 felony charges** and revealed all of the corruption, concealment, conspiracy, and fabrication committed by the top NC state officials. T. Vance Holloman was removed from his statewide position to a local town of Apex, NC. Beth Wood was also relieved of her duties by the governor as a result of the criminal acts she committed.

I was the first citizen of NC who was indicted with felony charges from OSA, then had ALL 17 felony charges dropped!! This had never happened before and I made history!! I believe this happened so I could help other innocent individuals who were falsely indicted and sent to prison.

I recommend that the current NC state auditor and current NC Attorney General go back and investigate those who were indicted and went to prison by Beth Wood, who was State Auditor at the time.

*For we wrestle not against flesh and blood, but against
principalities, against powers, against the rulers of the
darkness of this world, against spiritual wickedness in high
places. Wherefore take unto you the whole armour of God,
that ye may be able to withstand in the evil day,
and having done all, to stand.*
Ephesians 6:12-13 KJV

*Many are the afflictions of the righteous:
but the Lord delivereth him out of them all.*
Psalms 34:19 KJV

References

Opeka, T. (2023). "Wood's career as NC state auditor ends with sentencing on misdemeanor charges." The Carolina Journal. Retrieved from: https://www.carolinajournal.com/woods-career-as-nc-state-auditor-ends-with-sentencing-on-misdemeanor-charges/

Beau, M., Binker, M. (2013). "Princeville mayor indicted on embezzlement charges." WRAL News. Retrieved from: https://www.wral.com/story/princeville-mayor-indicted-on-embezzlement-charges/12747557/

United States Court of Appeals for the Fourth Circuit. Retrieved from: US Court of Appeals for 4th Circuit: chrome-extension://efaidnbmnnnibpcajpcglclefindmkaj/https://www.ca4.uscourts.gov/opinions/201093.U.pdf

Oates, et al v. North Carolina Department of State Treasurer, et al, No.5:2016cv00623 – Document 121 (E.D.N.C. 2017). Retrieved from: https://law.justia.com/cases/federal/district-courts/north-carolina/ncedce/5:2016cv00623/151350/121/

About the Author

Priscilla E. Oates is founder of Positive Generation in Christ, Inc., a behavioral health organization. Mrs. Oates imparted much of her passion for her community as co-founder of Positive Generation in Christ Altar Center's vision to teach, train, and equip mature believers for the ministry's work. She is also founder and CEO of POM Ministries, which enhances people to become productive citizens through conferences, workshops, media, and speaking engagements.

Born and raised in Princeville, North Carolina, she is the youngest of thirteen children. She is the daughter of the late Maggie and Julius (Sr.) Everette. Priscilla E. Oates was ordained into the ministry as Co-Pastor under the leadership of Pastor Duarthur Oates in 2002. She continues to empower the next generation by empowering citizens with jobs, training, and critical assistance in the same community where she grew up.

She attended and graduated in 1987 from NC A&T State University in Greensboro. NC and studied Accounting. She also studied Public Relations at East Carolina University in Greenville, North Carolina.

In 2002, Mrs. Oates became the youngest Black Mayor in the state of North Carolina. She served as the Mayor of Princeville, the oldest town in the United States of America chartered by Blacks. Prior to serving as Mayor, she served as a Princeville Commissioner in the year 2000. She was elected a second time in 2010 as Mayor of Princeville, North Carolina.

17 Felony Charges: NOT GUILTY

She is married to Duarthur Oates, Sr., and they are the proud parents of Duarthur Oates, Jr.

If you would like additional information or to connect with Priscilla E. Oates, please visit the website: https://www.pomministry.org/

Additional Books

If you would like to purchase all of the complete depositions, they will be available on Amazon!

TITLE:
Political Assassination on the Town of Princeville, North Carolina

Documents to Review

SCAN HERE to read the original press release by Attorney Charles Bonner, shown on page 77.

SCAN HERE to read the order of the Superior Court directly from Judge W. Osmond Smith, III, shown on page 79.

www.ingramcontent.com/pod-product-compliance
Lightning Source LLC
Chambersburg PA
CBHW060143150626
46550CB00014B/325